Integrating Python with Leading Computer Forensics Platforms

Integrating Python with Leading Computer Forensics Platforms

Chet Hosmer

Gary Kessler, Technical Editor

ELSEVIER

AMSTERDAM • BOSTON • HEIDELBERG • LONDON
NEW YORK • OXFORD • PARIS • SAN DIEGO
SAN FRANCISCO • SINGAPORE • SYDNEY • TOKYO

Syngress is an Imprint of Elsevier

SYNGRESS.

Syngress is an imprint of Elsevier
50 Hampshire Street, 5th Floor, Cambridge, MA 02139, United States

Notices
Knowledge and best practice in this field are constantly changing. As new research and experience
broaden our understanding, changes in research methods, professional practices, or medical treatment
may become necessary.

Practitioners and researchers must always rely on their own experience and knowledge in evaluating
and using any information, methods, compounds, or experiments described herein. In using such
information or methods they should be mindful of their own safety and the safety of others, including
parties for whom they have a professional responsibility.

To the fullest extent of the law, neither the Publisher nor the authors, contributors, or editors, assume
any liability for any injury and/or damage to persons or property as a matter of products liability,
negligence or otherwise, or from any use or operation of any methods, products, instructions, or ideas
contained in the material herein.

Library of Congress Cataloging-in-Publication Data
A catalog record for this book is available from the Library of Congress

British Library Cataloguing-in-Publication Data
A catalogue record for this book is available from the British Library

ISBN: 978-0-12-809949-0

For information on all Syngress publications
visit our website at https://www.elsevier.com/

Working together
to grow libraries in
developing countries

www.elsevier.com • www.bookaid.org

Publisher: Todd Green
Acquisition Editor: Chris Katsaropoulos
Editorial Project Manager: Anna Valutkevich
Production Project Manager: Priya Kumaraguruparan
Cover Designer: Mark Rogers

Typeset by SPi Global, India

To our incredible granddaughter Zoey Marie.

Contents

Author Biography

Chet Hosmer is the founder of Python Forensics, Inc., a nonprofit organization focused on the collaborative development of open-source investigative technologies using the Python programming language. He serves as a visiting professor at Utica College in the Cybersecurity Graduate program where his research and teaching focus on advanced steganography/data hiding methods and related defenses. He is also an adjunct faculty member at Champlain College in the Masters of Science in Digital Forensic Science Program where he is researching and working with the graduate students to advance the application Python to solve hard problems facing digital investigators.

Chet makes numerous appearances each year to discuss emerging cyber threats including National Public Radio's Kojo Nnamdi show, ABC's Primetime Thursday, NHK Japan, and ABC News Australia. He is also a frequent contributor to technical and news stories relating to cyber security and forensics and has been interviewed and quoted by IEEE, The New York Times, The Washington Post, Government Computer News, Salon.com, DFI News, and Wired Magazine.

Chet is the author of three recent Elsevier/Syngress Books: *Python Passive Network Mapping*: ISBN-13: 978-0128027219, *Python Forensics*: ISBN-13: 978-0124186767, and *Data Hiding* which is co/authored with Mike Raggo: ISBN-13: 978-1597497435. He delivers keynote and plenary talks on various cyber security-related topics around the world each year.

Preface

Modern digital forensic investigation platforms have evolved from simple command line tools to complete enterprise and mobile device investigation systems. This evolvement has provided standardization for the acquisition and analysis of forensic evidence collected from a variety of computers, networks, mobile devices, the cloud, and even the entire enterprise. This evolution has resulted in a rich set of proven investigative processes and procedures and has led to the creation of training and certification programs that ensure the resulting captured evidence will stand up to the scrutiny of our justice system.

The next step in the evolution is twofold.

It has become difficult for the vendors of these platforms to keep up with the almost daily demand for new requirements based on the introduction of new devices, the manifestation of new threats or challenges, the need for needed cooperation between organizations using different toolsets, and of course the continuous demand for faster processing of evidence. The first step toward the future is for those investigating cybercrime to offer enhancements to these platforms ranging from simple automation to new approaches to analyzing the resulting data collected by these platforms.

Second, the need to apply a wide range of algorithms, analytics, and semantics to the evidence collected by these platforms has become paramount. Today, the great work done by these platforms can be characterized as: accurate data acquisition, preservation of the acquired data, format and organization of the data, and display of the results. The next logical step is to open up the access to that data in order to perform additional processing, analysis, and semantic analysis and to provide greater insight into the meaning of what has been collected, preserved, organized, and formatted.

The purpose of this book is to demonstrate how this can be accomplished by integrating the Python programming language with selected platforms. The Python language not only provides an on-ramp for those new to software development but also serves more advanced developers based upon the wide ranging support available within and for Python. This book shows how additional processing can be accomplished by way of example using four very different digital forensic platforms that all have recognized the importance of opening access to their platforms. In addition, the platforms were chosen due to the diversity of the integration method needed for each. The approaches shown here, however, should provide the underpinnings necessary to apply similar methods and approaches to integration for other popular forensic platforms.

For those purchasing the book, access to all the source code presented is available at:

www.Python-Forensics.org

I look forwarding to collaborating with each of you.

Chet Hosmer

Acknowledgments

I would like to thank:

Gary Kessler for his insight and always supportive comments. I could not have a better technical editor; I'm looking forward to our next project.

Chris Katsaropoulos for his support and continued enthusiasm for my work and to the whole team at Elsevier for all the guidance, patience, and support along the way.

Kevin Delong for his encouragement for this project and assistance in providing all the required resources from Access Data and Syntricate.

Carlton Jeffcoat and the entire WetStone/Allen team for supporting this project and for providing the needed technology and guidance.

Brian Carrier for providing Autopsy and Sleuthkit to forensic investigators around the world and for adding a cool integration point for Python.

James Habben and the Guidance Software team for helping to build a gateway to Python from the EnCase platform.

To forensic investigators around the world that desire to add their own innovation to this field, and this book was written to directly support your endeavors.

And, finally, to my wife Janet for always supporting me regardless how crazy the idea might be.

## CHAPTER 1

Integrating Python With Forensics Platforms

INTRODUCTION

The Python programming language and environment has proven to be easy to learn and use, and is adaptable to virtually any domain or challenge problem. Companies such as Google, Dropbox, Disney, Industrial Light and Magic, and YouTube just to mention a handful are using Python within their operations. Additionally, organizations such as NASA's Jet Propulsion Lab, the National Weather Service, the Swedish Meteorological and Hydrological Institute (SMHI), and Lawrence Livermore National Laboratory rely on Python to build models, make predictions, run experiments, and control critical operational systems.

When integrating Python with computer forensic platforms, several areas can benefit:

(1) Automation of current manual processes
(2) Rapid prototyping of new examination methods
(3) Access to a rich library of packages that can accelerate the development of new approaches
(4) Enhanced performance by leveraging multiprocessing, set theory, dictionaries, and other advanced methods that are ideally suited to enhance forensic examination

For those new to Python, the best place to start is at the Python Software Foundation (PSF), website at www.python.org as depicted in Fig. 1.1.

WHAT IS THE PYTHON VALUE PROPOSITION FOR FORENSICS?

The use of scripting languages to enhance, modify, or meet new forensic challenges is not new. On the other hand, Python is not just another scripting language; it is a complete object-oriented software development environment that

1

Integrating Python with Leading Computer Forensics Platforms. http://dx.doi.org/10.1016/B978-0-12-809949-0.00001-7

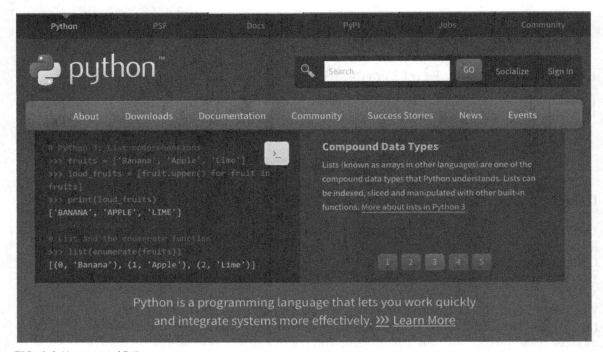

FIG. 1.1 Homepage of Python.org.

is built for rapid prototyping. In addition, Python is free, open source, cross platform and provides a much easier on-ramp to learn by novice developers and examiners with no previous programming or computer science background. In addition, the availability of free online resources, tutorials, and examples. Also, hundreds of books are available—from introductory level to quite advanced topics.

The Python language itself has several fundamental principals that can be best expressed by what is called the Zen of Python, which is expressed in the Python Enhancement Proposal number 20 or PEP 20 for short, by Tim Peters in 2004:

- Beautiful is better than ugly
- Explicit is better than implicit
- Simple is better than complex
- Complex is better than complicated
- Flat is better than nested
- Sparse is better than dense
- Readability counts
- Special cases aren't special enough to break the rules

- Although practicality beats purity
- Errors should never pass silently, unless explicitly silenced
- In the face of ambiguity, refuse the temptation to guess
- There should be one—and preferably only one—obvious way to do it. Although that way may not be obvious at first unless you're Dutch
- Now is better than never
- Although never is often better than *right* now
- If the implementation is hard to explain, it's a bad idea
- If the implementation is easy to explain, it may be a good idea

RESOURCES

If you are new to Python and/or programming and looking, or needing to delve a little deeper into Python programming, the following resources are provided to get you started. I have also included listings for some higher-level forensics-based Python texts.

Books

Automate the Boring Stuff With Python: Practical Programming for Total Beginners First Edition

By Al Sweigart

ISBN-10: 1593275994

ISBN-13: 978-1593275990

Learn how to write programs using Python to create code that can do in minutes what took hours to do by hand—without any prior programming experience. Walk through each program with step-by-step instructions and use your newfound skills on the challenges at the end of the chapter that build on the example.

Python: Learn Python in One Day and Learn It Well. Python for Beginners With Hands-on Project

By LCF Publishing and Jamie Chan

ISBN-10: 1506094384

ISBN-13: 978-1506094380

This book breaks down complex concepts, so you can easily understand the Python language and how to use it, even if you've never written a program before. All concepts are shown in the examples with output provided.

Python Crash Course: A Hands-On, Project-Based Introduction to Programming

By Eric Matthes

ISBN-10: 1593276036

ISBN-13: 978-1593276034

A thorough introduction to using Python for programming. You will be solving problems, writing programs, and making things work in no time. Learn about the concepts of basic programming like lists, classes, and dictionaries, and use them to write and test your code.

Python Forensics: A Workbench for Inventing and Sharing Digital Forensic Technology

By Chet Hosmer

ISBN-10: 0124186769

ISBN-13: 978-0124186767

Python forensics provides many never-before-published proven forensic modules, libraries, and solutions that can be used right out of the box. In addition, detailed instruction and documentation provided with the code samples will allow even novice Python programmers to add their own unique twists or use the models presented to build new solutions.

Violent Python: A Cookbook for Hackers, Forensic Analysts, Penetration Testers, and Security Engineers

By TJ O'Connor

ISBN-10: 1597499579

ISBN-13: 978-1597499576

Violent Python takes theoretical offensive computing concepts and shows you how to implement them for practical applications. Demonstrates how to write scripts in Python to accomplish a number of offensive tasks, ranging from data mining to scripting an attack utilizing common Python code.

Online Resources and Tutorials

One only has to type "Python language" into any search engine to be presented with scores of websites offering help, tutorials, and documentation along with free code. A few that stand out for those who are not familiar with programming and/or Python are listed here.

learnpython.org
Whether you are an experienced programmer or not, this website is intended for everyone who wishes to learn the Python programming language. Learn the basics or view advanced tutorials.

python.org/about/gettingstarted/
Information throughout this site is provided by the PSF and offers comprehensive resource materials for installing and using Python at all levels.

The mission of the PSF is to promote, protect, and advance the Python programming language, and to support and facilitate the growth of a diverse and international community of Python programmers. This is the official site for Python including free downloads, documentation, and developer information.

CS for All: Introduction to Computer Science and Python Programming
This is a fun, fast-paced introduction to solving interesting problems with computer science through Python programming. Offered through *edx.org*, this free tutorial, along with others found on this site, provides a good understanding of how to work with the language https://www.cs.hmc.edu/csforall/.

Formal Courses

For those looking for a more formal education that includes Python, here are a few colleges and universities that teach courses in Python as of the publishing of this book. I should mention the *Communications of the ACM*, a monthly journal that was established in 1957 and is still today the recognized authority on the latest research and trends in computer science. They published an article in the March 2015 issue entitled: "Python for Beginners." Among other things, this article discusses how and why Python is being taught as the first language to freshman computer science students at universities such as Carnegie Mellon, MIT, Cal Berkeley, and Georgia Tech.

Introduction to Python for Data Science, Microsoft
https://www.edx.org/course/introduction-python-data-science-microsoft-dat208x
A Gentle Introduction to Programming Using Python, MIT
http://ocw.mit.edu/courses/electrical-engineering-and-computer-science/6-189-a-gentle-introduction-to-programming-using-python-january-iap-2011/index.htm
Python Programming EL ENG X442.3, UC Berkeley
http://extension.berkeley.edu/search/publicCourseSearchDetails.do?method=load&courseId=40968

Introduction to Computing and Programming in Python, Georgia Tech
http://lorraine.gatech.edu/introduction-computing-and-programming-python
DFS 510—Scripting For Digital Forensics, Champlain College
http://catalog.champlain.edu/preview_course_nopop.php?catoid=11&coid=8585
CS 1110: Introduction to Computing Using Python, Cornell University
http://www.cs.cornell.edu/Courses/cs1110/2014sp/materials/python.php
Programming for Everybody (Getting Started With Python), University of Michigan
https://www.coursera.org/learn/python

WHAT ARE THE POSSIBLE INTEGRATION POINTS AND METHODS?

One of the most important considerations when integrating Python into the investigative process, or more specifically into a specific platform, is determining possible integration points.

There are many ways to approach this, but let's review the most obvious options:

(A) Preprocessing
(B) Postprocessing
(C) Direct Application programming interface (API) integration
(D) Secondary information gathering
(E) Secondary processing of hard problems

Preprocessing

When interfacing with many of the modern forensic platforms, examiners need to supply quality information when setting up tools for use. This typically comes in the form of inputs to the case such as keywords, names, places, phone numbers along with times, and dates of specific events. Creating these input files whether they are simple text lists, comma-separated value (CSV) files in a specific format, eXtensible Markup Language (XML) input files, or other proprietary formats is a tedious process. Python can assist examiners in several ways:

(1) Provide a method to input
(2) Validate the entries (ensuring both format, elimination of duplicate entries, etc.)
(3) Provide a method for storing and managing these files

Then the examiners can reach back to these files when ready to supply these data to the forensic tools, update this information, and even convert this input to alternate formats if more than one forensic tool is being utilized.

Postprocessing

When traditional forensic tools process a case or device (storage device, memory snapshot, cell phone, tablet, network activity, etc.), they generate or have the ability export certain elements for deeper examination. A simple example would be a jpeg image that requires additional or more detailed examination. In this case, Python scripts can easily provide that deeper or custom examination of the resulting image or memory snapshot. Once these secondary Python scripts have completed their analysis, the results would then be integrated back into the main case, which would likely include examiner comments, notes, and observations.

Direct API Integration

In some cases, forensic platforms have an application interface that provides a direct method of connecting 3rd party tools and scripts to the main platform. Typically, this provides 3rd party scripts read access to data already processed by the forensic platform. For example, Guidance Software EnCase utilizes EnScript, its own scripting language, which is used to process case information directly or it can be used as a gateway to other 3rd party scripts. This method more tightly couples the Python script with the forensic platform and can also provide a direct method of adding new results and observations directly into the case.

Secondary Information Gathering

Another area where Python can provide value to the examiner is by developing scripts that utilize case data to gather secondary information regarding suspects, phone numbers, locations, social networking, etc. In this example, information provided as an output from the forensic platform could lead to extraction of data from various Internet related sources providing collateral data. For example:

- Automation of the phone numbers locations
- Mapping of geolocation data collected from the metadata of photographs
- Compiling lists of associates and activities from Facebook, Linkedin, Twitter, and Instagram accounts
- Identification of people in photographs
- Mapping of identified postal codes to specific locations

Secondary Processing of Hard Problems

In many cases, the ability to perform the processing on hard problems is difficult to execute from within the forensics platforms themselves and instead needs to be executed separately. Some of these applications include:

(1) Processing images or multimedia files that may contain hidden data (i.e., steganography)
(2) Brute force cracking of encrypted files
(3) Generation of salted Rainbow tables
(4) Analysis of collections (images, documents, multimedia files)
(5) Correlation of evidence across a diverse set of cases

In this context, **Steganography** refers to the hiding of information within digital carrier files such as images and multimedia files. The concept is to make slight alterations of the content of these carrier files that does not distort their normal rendering or output.

Rainbow tables are typically large precomputed lists of cryptographic hash values of passwords or keys. If the cryptographic hash value is known, then the Rainbow table can be used to lookup the password associated with the specific hash value.

WHY OPEN SOURCE?

There has been a long running debate whether open source solutions provide any advantage when performing forensic investigations. The following sidebar is an excerpt from "Python Forensics, A Workbench for Inventing and Sharing Digital Forensic Technology," Syngress 2014—a book I authored.

Excerpt taken from Python forensics, by Chet Hosmer

In 2003 Brian Carrier [Carrier] published a paper that examined rules of evidence standards including Daubert, and compared and contrasted the open source and closed source forensic tools. One of his key conclusions was, "Using the guidelines of the Daubert tests, we have shown that open source tools may more clearly and comprehensively meet the guideline requirements than would closed source tools.

The results are not automatic of course, just because the source is open. Rather, specific steps must be followed regarding design, development, and validation.

1. Can the program or algorithm be explained? This explanation should be explained in words, not only in code.
2. Has the script been independently validated?

3. Has enough information been provided such that thorough tests can be developed to test the program?
4. Have error rates been calculated and validated independently?
5. Has the program been studied and peer reviewed?
6. Has the program been generally accepted by the community?

The real question is how can Python-developed forensic scripts that extend the capabilities of forensic platforms meet these objectives? Chapters 3–7 will introduce several specific Python scripts that enhance or extend specific forensic platforms: During the development of these new integrated methods, the following criteria will be considered and applied:

1. Clear definition of the challenge problem. In other words, what problem are we trying to solve?
2. Clear definition of the objectives of the Python-based approach.
3. Considerations for the test sets necessary to validate the approach.
4. Algorithm description (English readable).
5. Code development and walk-through.
6. Involving the community (When plausible).

WHAT FORENSIC PLATFORMS ARE COVERED?

The next consideration is what forensic platforms should be covered in this book. Looking at the landscape of forensic platforms, many are worthy of inclusion; however, it is not feasible to include them all. Rather, it is important to select a sampling that covers a range of platform that allow for the development of Python scripts that utilize different methods of integration. The following table lists the platforms, the developer, and the corresponding chapter covering integration into those platforms.

Forensic Platform	Developer	Chapter Coverage
MPE+	Access Data	Chapter 3
EnCase	Guidance Software	Chapter 4
US-LATT	WetStone Technologies	Chapter 5
Autopsy	Brian Carrier	Chapter 6

KEYS TO SUCCESS

As we examine the landscape of forensic platforms, it is certain that they are likely to change, expand, evolve, or even be replaced by new solutions or approaches. Depending upon the type of integration we are attempting (preprocessing, postprocessing, direct API integration, secondary information gathering, or the processing of hard problems), different methods may be necessary. However, several key considerations should be observed when developing integration methods regardless of the approach taken.

(1) Do not impact the evidence of the case held by the forensic platform. You can add content in the form of reports and observations, but never modify or remove evidence.

(2) The Python scripts should first be developed to be standalone, meaning that inputs to the scripts utilize standard command line options. Even when platforms utilize and API, we should always unit test the core capabilities of the scripts prior to integration.

(3) The Python scripts should be fully tested prior to integration and consider failure modes carefully to ensure that they will fail "gracefully" once integrated with forensic platforms.

(4) Document in great detail the scripts objectives, design, and implementation. This will ensure that future modifications, adaptations, testing, and possible testimony to the efficacy of the script will be solid.

(5) Understand and carefully consider the different possible methods of integration and choose a method that allows for the greatest control over the processing.

(6) Create test sets that cover a broad range of possible conditions which include possible error conditions. A simple example would be if your script is processing JPEG images, make sure your test sets include invalid JPEGs, files that claim to be JPEGs but are not, non-JPEG images, and nonimage files.

(7) Ensure that the output or results of the scripts provide clear details, including data source and date/time.

(8) Ensure that the output includes a forensic log that includes details of the processing performed by the script.

(9) Ensure that the date and time of the computer running the script is synchronized with an official source and documented.

(10) Ensure that information such as the script version, author, investigator, and case identifying information are included in the output of the script.

(11) Test, test, test, and retest before processing actual case data.

Following these steps will ensure that when (not if) integration with forensic platforms changes, your ability to adapt your scripts to integration methods will be straightforward.

REVIEW

In this chapter, we outlined the objectives of the book, provided additional resources for further study and learning of Python. The chapter also addresses the value proposition for using an open source programming language for forensic applications. In addition, we identified the specific forensic platforms that will be covered in this text. We also identified the key integration points that will be considered for each platform. Finally, we provided some of the key considerations or guidelines for the successful integration of Python scripts with forensic platforms today and in the future.

Additional Resources

[1] Carrier B. Open source digital forensic tools—the legal argument. Digital-Evidence.org. Available from: http://www.digital-evidence.org/papers/opensrc_legal.pdf; 2003.

[2] Hosmer C. Python Forensics: a workbench for inventing and sharing digital forensic technology. Waltham, MA: Syngress; 2014, ISBN 978-0124186767.

[3] The Official Site for everything Python, Python Software Foundation, www.python.org.

## CHAPTER 2

Key Python Language Elements for Forensics

INTRODUCTION

The Python Standard Library and most all 3rd party libraries are vast and diverse. As we discussed in Chapter 1, there are many resources for learning the Python language (books, tutorials, websites, formal education, etc.). These resources, however, tend to be broadly focused on teaching the language in general. For those of you out there who are not planning a career in Computer Science, there needs to be a faster on-ramp for getting work done within their respective domains.

Fortunately for us, there are specific elements of the Python language, its libraries and considerations that are unique, important, and directly relevant to digital investigations and forensics. In addition, for those with limited experience with Python, scripting or programming in general, some basic language introduction is in order, especially to avoid some common pitfalls or misunderstandings about the language.

Many times when giving a presentation, code demonstration or teaching a class on Python someone will raise their hand and say, "I understand what you just did and how you did it, but how did you know to approach the problem in that manner?" I usually answer that question first by saying, "That's a great question!", because many of us that have been developing software for decades inherently know a good number of ways to approach a specific software problem. That knowledge simply comes with experience. But, how and where do you start if you don't have decades of experience?

One of the biggest problems newcomers to Python—or more specifically newcomers to applying Python to forensics or incident response—have is that they sit down with one of the general Python texts and are immediately frustrated because it is difficult to make the connection from the general programming examples provided to the specifics of what they want to accomplish. The beauty of using Python is that it is all about getting things done, not about dealing with the intricacies of the language. That comes with practice, patience, and success. Therefore, instead of providing you with yet another language reference, I'm

Integrating Python with Leading Computer Forensics Platforms. http://dx.doi.org/10.1016/B978-0-12-809949-0.00002-9

going to walk you through several examples that are relevant to digital investigation, forensics, and incident response. I'll provide you with my reasoning regarding specific challenges and then show you how I would develop solutions to those challenges with the Python language, explaining each step of the process along the way. Just one caveat before I get started, there are many ways to approach problems in Python or other languages for that matter, so keep in mind that there are likely a myriad of other ways to solve the specific challenges I present.

Font Usage

I like to keep the font usage simple when depicting Python code, typed commands, and script output.

Python code, variables, function names : Courier New Italic
Python Output : Lucida Console
Typed Commands : Lucida Console Bold

QUICK OVERVIEW OF THE PYTHON ENVIRONMENT

The first step of course is getting Python and a development environment established on your computer(s). For many of you that are using Macs or common Linux distributions, Python is already installed and ready to go. If you are a Windows user or wish to upgrade the default installation on your Mac or Linux distribution, then you will need to install Python. The best way to do that is to visit www.python.org/downloads/ as shown in Fig. 2.1. The python.org/download/ page will detect your platform and present you with a download option

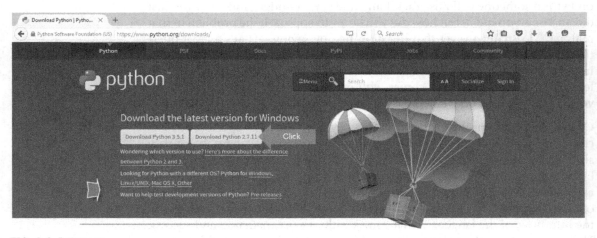

FIG. 2.1 Python.org.

for your computer. As you notice, as of this writing you have two basic options… either Python 3.5.1 and 2.7.11. So, you have a choice to make here since this book is written for 2.7.×. To provide an easier on-ramp, selecting this option will ensure that the book examples and downloadable source code will work straight out of the box.

Installing Python for Windows

Once you have selected the version for download (assuming that you are installing using Microsoft), you will be prompted to save the associated .msi (Microsoft Installer package) as shown in Fig. 2.2.

FIG. 2.2 Saving the selected Microsoft Installer package.

Once the .msi package is downloaded, navigate to the systems download folder as shown in Fig. 2.3. Then double click the installation package to launch the installer.

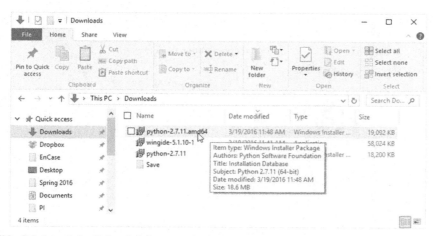

FIG. 2.3 Launch the Python installer.

This action will launch the Python Installer and walk you through the installation process as shown in Figs. 2.4–2.9. Take special note regarding Figs. 2.6 and 2.7 and make sure that the pip selection and the path selection are both set to "entire feature will be installed on the local hard drive" as shown. This will ensure that Python is included in the Windows path and that the pip (the Python package management system) is installed. The pip command is used to install and manage software packages in Python.

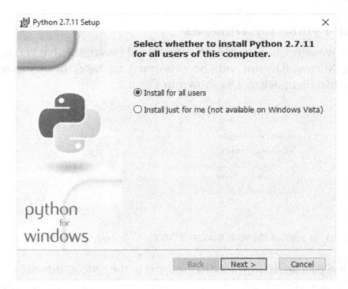

FIG. 2.4 Select user access to Python.

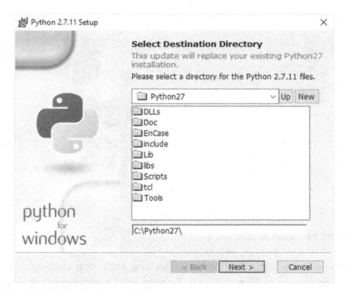

FIG. 2.5 Select the Python destination folder.

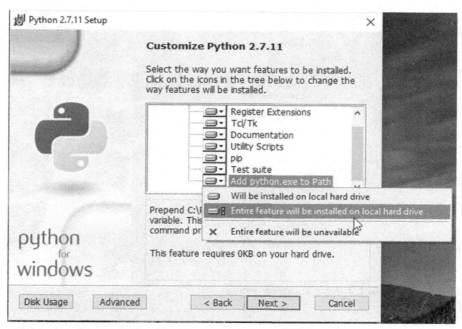

FIG. 2.6 Ensure Python is added to the windows path.

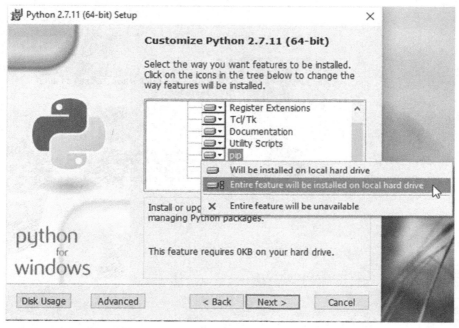

FIG. 2.7 Ensure Python package management (pip) is installed.

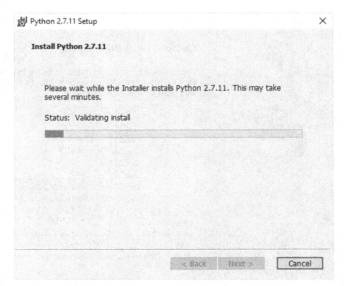

FIG. 2.8 Python installation progress.

FIG. 2.9 Python installation completed select finish.

Once the installation process is completed, you can quickly ensure that Python is ready to run. Simply launch the Windows Command Line (Note: launching the command line will be specific to your platform depending on the version of Windows that you are using). Once the command line is up and running, type the command *python* as shown in Fig. 2.10. This will launch the Python interpreter and display the current version. You will see the Python prompt which is three greater than symbols: $>>>$. At this point I like to enter the simplest Python command:

print "Hello Universe"

If Python is installed and working correctly, the interpreter should respond as shown in Fig. 2.10. To exit Python (on a Windows Computer), press ctrl-C.

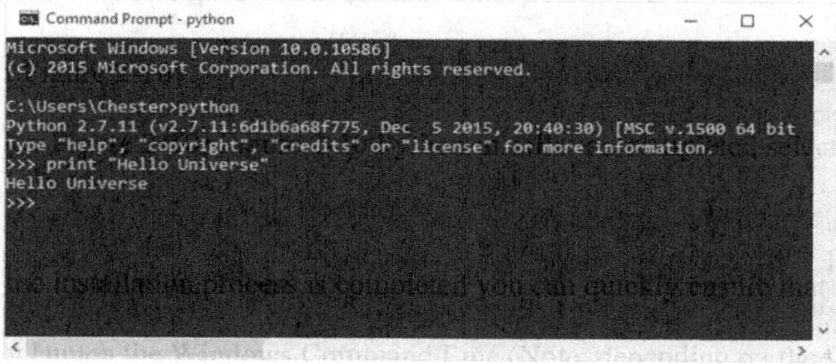

FIG. 2.10 Verify the installation via the window command line.

Setting Up a Python Integrated Development Environment

The next step in the process is to install a Python Integrated Development Environment (IDE). Several popular IDE's exist including:

IDLE:	Included with Python
PyCharm:	http://www.jetbrains.com/pycharm/
WingIDE:	http://www.wingware.com
Spyder:	https://pythonhosted.org/spyder/

and many more …

I use WingIDE by Wingware exclusively and will be using this IDE throughout the book as I have in my past books and publications. WingIDE supports Windows, Mac OS X, and Linux. It also can debug Python code remotely (e.g., I use this feature when debugging code running on a Raspberry Pi). Wingware offers a 30-day free trial as well, so you can try before you purchase.

Fig. 2.11 depicts the current home page for Wingware offering a free download as identified in the upper right-hand corner of the screenshot. Clicking the button takes you directly to the download page.

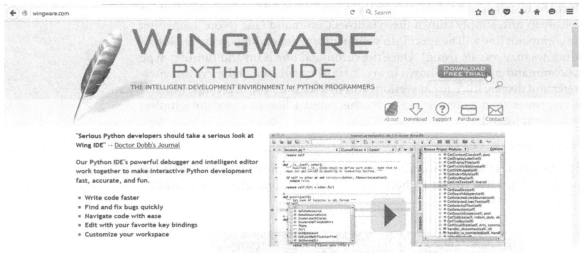

FIG. 2.11 Wingware home page—free download.

Wingware offers the same free download for all of their versions, thus taking the Professional version for a test drive seems like a good place to start. Fig. 2.12 highlights the recommended download link for the Professional version.

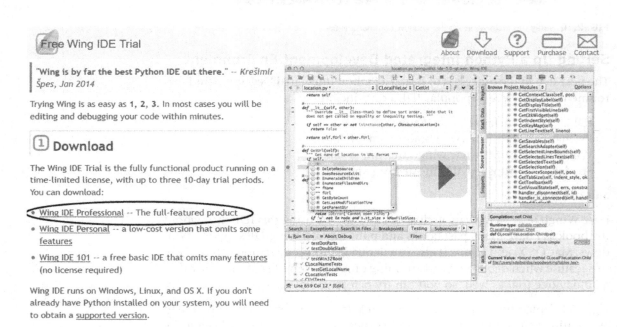

FIG. 2.12 WingIDE professional version download link.

Based on the platform you are running (in my case Windows 10 for this example), Wingware will provide you the download options most suited for your platform. In this case, they recommended the Windows Installer 32 or 64 bit (see Fig. 2.13).

FIG. 2.13 WingIDE platform selection.

Clicking the selection will directly download the Windows Installer as shown in Fig. 2.14.

FIG. 2.14 Downloading WingIDE.

Next, you can navigate to your download folder and then select and launch the installer as shown in Fig. 2.15.

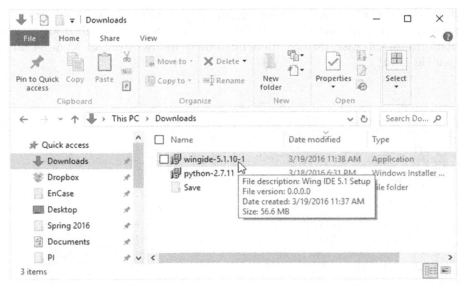

FIG. 2.15 Launching the WingIDE installer.

The installer performs all the installation operations (as shown in Fig. 2.16).

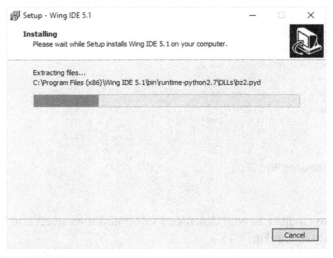

FIG. 2.16 WingIDE installing.

Fig. 2.17 depicts the completed installation.

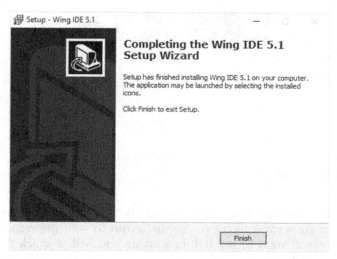

FIG. 2.17 WingIDE installation complete.

I prefer to add WingIDE to the Windows Taskbar for easy access. Note that adding applications to the taskbar in Windows is different for each version. Fig. 2.18 depicts the Windows 10 method. Fig. 2.19 shows the WingIDE feather Icon on the Windows Taskbar. Fig. 2.20 depicts the WingIDE splash screen upon selection from the Taskbar.

FIG. 2.18 Adding WingIDE to the windows taskbar.

FIG. 2.19 WingIDE taskbar icon.

FIG. 2.20 WingIDE splash screen.

Fig. 2.21 depicts a typical layout of WingIDE. The Integrated Development Environment allows you to customize the layout to your preferences. I have numbered several areas of the IDE to provide you with a quick tour of the important capabilities of the IDE.

[1] This is the Main Menu bar providing access to the major functions within the IDE (i.e., opening and closing of Projects or Files) and including common editing features such as copy, cut, paste, find, and replace. Debugging actions such as running the Python scripting, stepping over instructions, stepping into function, setting and clearing breakpoints are also accessed from this menu. The professional version has built-in testing and unit testing features in order to validate and regression test your scripts. This can be quite important when developing forensic scripts. WingIDE has extensive help and tutorials built directly into the IDE, including not only help associated with WingIDE but also access to the Python 2.7.11 manual set.

[2] Window 2 contains the contents of the currently open and selected file. WingIDE can maintain access to numerous files that are part of, or independent of, the project you are currently working on. In this example, the window contains the contents of the file PyTest.py, which is a simple Python script containing 7 lines of source code (line numbers are depicted in the left most column). Line 1 contains the command *print "Hello Universe"* instructing the interpreter to print the string Hello Universe to the standard output. Line 2 is blank. Line 3 creates a variable named *myString* which will take on the contents of the string "This is a test of the Python WingIDE Environment," by using the assignment operator = or the equal sign. Line 4 is blank. Line 5 uses the *print* command instructing the interpreter to print the contents of the string *myString* to standard output. Line 6 is blank. Line 7 instructs the interpreter to *print* the string "*Test Complete*" to standard output.

[3] You notice a dot to the left of the contents of Line 7, and the script line is highlighted. The dot indicates a breakpoint is set instructing the program to halt *prior* to the execution of this line of code.

[4] This tabbed window has many capabilities. Currently, the Debug I/O tab is selected. The contents of this window are displayed showing the output from the running script, which is currently stopped prior to the execution of line 7.

[5] This tabbed window depicts a variety of data associated with the running script. The tab currently selected is "stack data," which displays the current local and global variables associated with the running script. For example, you see the contents of the variable *myString*, and the variable __*file*__ contains the name of the currently opened and running script.

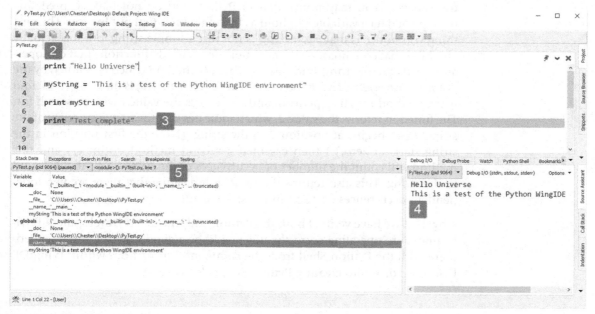

FIG. 2.21 WingIDE standard desktop with annotations.

Fig. 2.22 examines the Python Shell Tab found in Section 4. The Python shell tab provides direct access to the Python Shell with the IDE. This provides users with the ability to experiment with the Python language without the need to develop a new script or a complete program. It is a great way to become familiar with the Python language, its data types, built-in functions, the Python Standard Library or to experiment with 3rd party libraries before putting them to use in complete programs.

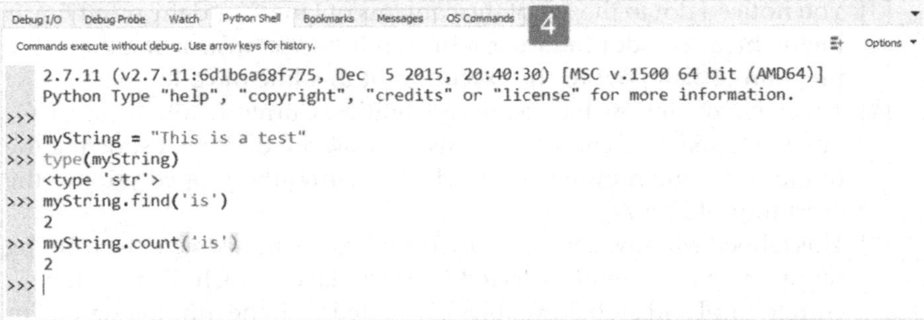

```
Debug I/O    Debug Probe    Watch    Python Shell    Bookmarks    Messages    OS Commands    4                                   ▼
Commands execute without debug.  Use arrow keys for history.                                                      ⯮⯮  Options ▼
    2.7.11 (v2.7.11:6d1b6a68f775, Dec  5 2015, 20:40:30) [MSC v.1500 64 bit (AMD64)]
    Python Type "help", "copyright", "credits" or "license" for more information.
>>>
>>> myString = "This is a test"
>>> type(myString)
    <type 'str'>
>>> myString.find('is')
    2
>>> myString.count('is')
    2
>>> |
```

FIG. 2.22 WingIDE Python shell in action.

In this example, I used the Python Shell to create a new variable named *myString*. I then used the built-in function *type()* to evaluate the type of the variable. You may notice that in Python you do not have to predefine the type of data a variable can hold as Python figures that out for you. The next thing you notice is that *myString* is not just a simple string, but it is actually an object that contains a plethora of built-in methods/functions that can operate directly on the string. I first use the *find()* method which is denoted by the dot notation *myString.find('is')* where *myString* is the object and .find is the method I wish to perform and *('is')* is the value I wish to search for. The function returns the value 2, which indicates that the first occurrence of the string *'is'* begins at position 2 in the string. (Note the first position in the string starts at zero.) I then executed a second method *count()*, and this method will count the number of occurrences of the string *'is'* that is found in the string. This also returns the value 2, indicating that there are two independent occurrences of *'is'* in the string *myString*.

Now that we have verified both the Python and Integrated Development Environment are operating correctly; this would be a good time for you to experiment with the Python Shell from the command line or from within WingIDE before we dive into creating Python Scripts for Forensics.

PYTHON FORENSICS SOURCE CODE TEMPLATE
SRC-2-1.PY

Now that you have experimented with the Python and Integrated Development Environments, let's examine a template Python Forensics script that you can use and reuse. The basic template does very little forensics work but rather provides a baseline structure for upcoming scripts. I have broken the script down into sections and will describe each section and then demonstrate the execution and output generated by the template.

Script SRC-2-1.1py

```python
'''
Copyright (c) 2016 Chet Hosmer

Permission is hereby granted, free of charge, to any person obtaining a copy
of this software and associated documentation files (the "Software"), to deal
in the Software without restriction, including without limitation the rights
to use, copy, modify, merge, publish, distribute, sublicense,
and/or sell copies of the Software, and to permit persons to whom the
Software is furnished to do so, subject to the following conditions:

The above copyright notice and this permission notice shall be included in
all copies or substantial portions of the Software.

Script Purpose: Forensic Template SRC-2-1
Script Version: 1.0
Script Author:  C.Hosmer

Script Revision History:
Version 1.0 March 2016

'''
```

```python
# Script Module Importing

# Python Standard Library Modules
import os              # Operating/Filesystem Module
import time            # Basic Time Module
import logging         # Script Logging

# Import 3rd Party Modules

# End of Script Module Importing
```

```python
# Script Constants

'''
Python does not support constants directly
however, by initializing variables here and
specifying them as UPPER_CASE you can make your
intent known
'''
# General Constants
SCRIPT_NAME    = "Script: Forensic Example Script One SRC-2-1"
SCRIPT_VERSION = "Version 1.0"
SCRIPT_AUTHOR  = "Author: C. Hosmer, Python Forensics"
SCRIPT_LOG     = "./FORENSIC_LOG.txt"

# LOG Constants used as input to LogEvent Function
LOG_DEBUG = 0              # Debugging Event
LOG_INFO  = 1              # Information Event
LOG_WARN  = 2              # Warning Event
LOG_ERR   = 3              # Error Event
LOG_CRIT  = 4              # Critical Event
LOG_OVERWRITE = True       # Set this contstant to True if the
                           # SCRIPT_LOG should be overwritten,
                           # False if not

# End of Script Constants
```

```
# Initialize the Forensic Log

try:
    # If LOG should be overwritten before
    # each run, the remove the old log
    if LOG_OVERWRITE:
        # Verify that the log exists before removing
        if os.path.exists(SCRIPT_LOG):
            os.remove(SCRIPT_LOG)

    # Initialize the Log include the Level and message
    logging.basicConfig(filename=SCRIPT_LOG,
format='%(levelname)s\t:%(message)s', level=logging.DEBUG)

except:
    print "Failed to initialize Logging"
    quit()

# End of Forensic Log Initialization
```

D

```
# Script Functions
'''
If your script will contain functions then insert them
here, before the execution of the main script.  This
will ensure that the functions will be callable from
anywhere in your script
'''

# Function: GetTime()
#
# Returns a string containing the current time
#
# Script uses the local system clock, time, date and timezone
# to calcuate the current time.  Thus sync your system
# clock before using this script
#
# Input: timeStyle = 'UTC', 'LOCAL', function will default to
#                    UTC Time if you pass in nothing.

def GetTime(timeStyle = "UTC"):

    if timeStyle == 'UTC':
        return ('UTC Time:', time.asctime(time.gmtime(time.time())))
    else:
        return ('LOC Time:', time.asctime(time.localtime(time.time())))

# End GetTime Function
```

E

```
# Function: LogEvent()
#
# Logs the event message and specified type
# Input:
#          eventType: LOG_INFO, LOG_WARN, LOG_ERR, LOG_CRIT or
#                       LOG_DEBUG
#          eventMessage : string containing the message to be
#                            logged


def LogEvent(eventType, eventMessage):

    try:

        timeStr = GetTime('UTC')
        # Combine current Time with the eventMessage
        # You can specify either 'UTC' or 'LOCAL'
        # Based on the GetTime parameter

        eventMessage = str(timeStr)+": "+eventMessage

        if eventType == LOG_INFO:
            logging.info(eventMessage)

        elif eventType == LOG_DEBUG:
            logging.debug(eventMessage)

        elif eventType == LOG_WARN:
            logging.warning(eventMessage)

        elif eventType == LOG_ERR:
            logging.error(eventMessage)

        elif eventType == LOG_CRIT:
            logging.critical(eventMessage)

        else:
            logging.info(eventMessage)
    except:
        print "Event Logging Failed"

# End LogEvent Function

# End of Script Functions
```

F

G
```python
# Script Classes
'''
If you script will contain classes then insert them
here, before the execution of the main script.  This
will ensure that the functions will be accessible from
anywhere in your script
'''

# End of Script Classes
```

H
```python
# Main Script Starts Here

LogEvent(LOG_INFO, SCRIPT_NAME)
LogEvent(LOG_INFO, SCRIPT_VERSION)
LogEvent(LOG_INFO, "Script Started")

# Print Basic Script Information

print SCRIPT_NAME
print SCRIPT_VERSION
print SCRIPT_AUTHOR

utcTime = GetTime()
print "Script Started: ", utcTime

#
# Script Work
# for the template we just sleep 5 seconds
#

print "Performing Work"
time.sleep(5)

utcTime = GetTime('UTC')
print "Script    Ended: ", utcTime

LogEvent(LOG_DEBUG, 'Test Debug')
LogEvent(LOG_WARN,  'Test Warning')
LogEvent(LOG_ERR,   'Test Error')
LogEvent(LOG_CRIT,  'Test Critical')

LogEvent(LOG_INFO,  'Script Ended')

# End of Script Main
```

A The section provides a place for you to include your copyright notice regarding the script. Since Python is intended to be an open source language, I have chosen this copyright notice for all the scripts that I develop. Your situation may differ and the restrictions for use and distribution may also differ. However, you should clearly define this section if you intend for others to utilize and share your code.

B The next section defines external Python modules that will be imported into our script. I have broken this section down into two parts. Part one is Python Standard Library modules that will be used. Part two is 3rd Party modules. This template only uses Python Standard Library Modules. The script imports the os, time, and logging modules.

os: The os module contains miscellaneous operating system interfaces. For example, use this if you wish to determine if a file or path exists, if you wish to navigate the filesystem or obtain the names of files. All of these are methods that are useful when examining the file system.

time: As the name implies, the time access and conversion module provide access to the system time and various useful conversions. This will assist us in recording various times during our forensics scripts.

logging: This module provides access to the built-in logging methods that will enable us to create a detailed log of any and all the actions we take.

Importing these modules provides us with access to all the methods and attributes associated with them. For a more detailed look at the Python Standard Library Modules, you can visit the Python Software Foundation documentation at: https://docs.python.org/2/library/index.html.

C The next section defines any constants that you will be using throughout your script. Python is a loosely typed language and as such, constants are not really constants, since they can be changed within your code, they are typically referred to as pseudo constants. A way to separate the pseudo constants from variables is how you define them. In the case of constants, I use all capital letters and separate words with the underscore character. For example, *SCRIPT_NAME* is a string of characters that is meant to represent the name of the script and should not be changed.

```
SCRIPT_NAME  = "Script: Forensic Example Script One SRC-2-1"
```

D In order to provide the entire script access to logging capabilities, this section initializes logging operations. You may have noticed in the constants section *SCRIPT_LOG* is defined as:

```
SCRIPT_LOG  = "./FORENSIC_LOG.txt"
```

This defines the pseudo constant for the name of the file where the log events are to be written. The notation here directs the log to be written in the current working directory, or in our case where the script is executed from. You may also notice that the forward slash (/) is used to define the path per the Unix/Linux convention, whereas Windows uses a backward slash (\) to delineate directories. Python will handle this properly for Windows and non-Windows environments. The value of using the forward slash is that it eliminates confusion with the backward slash that is used as an escape character; in Python, if you wish to use a backward slash in file and folder names, you must then use a double backslash (e.g., '.\\FORENSIC_LOG.TXT').

An additional constant was defined here relating to log actions: *LOG_OVER-WRITE = True* denotes whether the log file should be overwritten each time the script is run. If the constant is set to *True*, the log will be overwritten, and if the constant is set to *False*, data will be appended to the existing log file. Thus before the log is initialized, two tests are performed. First, the pseudo constant *LOG_OVERWRITE* is examined. If the value is set to True, the existence of a SCRIPT_LOG file is tested. If this evaluates to *True*, the *os.remove(SCRIPT_LOG)* method is utilized to delete the previously stored log file.

Using the:

```
logging.basicConfig(filename=SCRIPT_LOG,
format='%(levelname)s\t:%(message)s', level=logging.DEBUG)
```

method forensic logging is initialized. Many options exist when initializing the log. This example includes just the level that is specified (DEBUG, INFO, WARNING, ERROR, or CRITICAL) along with the specified message. In the upcoming 'Section F,' the details pertaining to the function that writes messages to the log will be covered.

E This next section of the Python Forensic template is set aside for defining local functions that will be included and accessible within the script. In this example, Sections E and F encompass the local function section and define the two local functions. Section E defines the local function:

```
def GetTime(timeStyle = "UTC"):
```

This function definition contains a couple of important aspects of writing solid forensic software. First, the function name is defined as *GetTime*. This type is considered camelcase where the first letter of each word in the function name is capitalized and lowercase is used for the remaining letters of the function name. Thus if we are consistent in our use, we can always distinguish function names from psuedo constants and variables. In this example, we also define a variable *timeStyle* that can be optionally passed into the function from the caller. You notice that *timeStyle* also use camel case; however, the first word is lower case then subsequent words are capitalized. Therefore, at a glance, it can quickly be determined that:

SCRIPT_LOG	is a psuedo constant
GetTime	is a function name
timeStyle	is a variable

The *GetTime* function simplifies the access to the time functions provided by the time module. The function returns a string representing the current time either in UTC or in Local Time conversions. Note the *GetTime* function uses the system time, date, and time zone to perform the appropriate conversions. Therefore, it is important that you synchronize your system time source prior to execution of the script.

If you would like to obtain time from an official source in Python, you can check out Chapter 6 in my previous book, *Python Forensics, A Workbench for Inventing and Sharing Digital Forensic Technology*.

F The second function within the local function section is:

LogEvent (eventType, eventMessage): This function requires two parameters ... the *eventType* and the *eventMessage*. The possible event types are defined in the constant section and the *eventMessage* is any string that you wish to have included in the log file. The function concatenates the current time (either UTC or Local time) with the passed message and then based on the specified *eventType* provided, uses the specified logging method to write the message to the log. If the *eventType* provided is not valid, the function will record the message as an INFO event.

G Section G is where any local class definition would be included. This simple template does not include any local classes, but future examples will; therefore, this provides just a placeholder.

H The last section is the main script section. For this template script, only a few simple actions are performed.

(1) Post several events to the forensic log
(2) Print several messages to the standard output
(3) Get and print the starting time of the script
(4) Sleep for a few seconds
(5) Get and print the ending time of the script

Executing SRC-2-1

The script can be executed either from within the IDE or from the command line, and the generated log file can be examined. Fig. 2.23 demonstrates the template script SRC-2-1.py executed from the Windows command line and also includes the resulting content of the FORENSIC_LOG.TXT file.

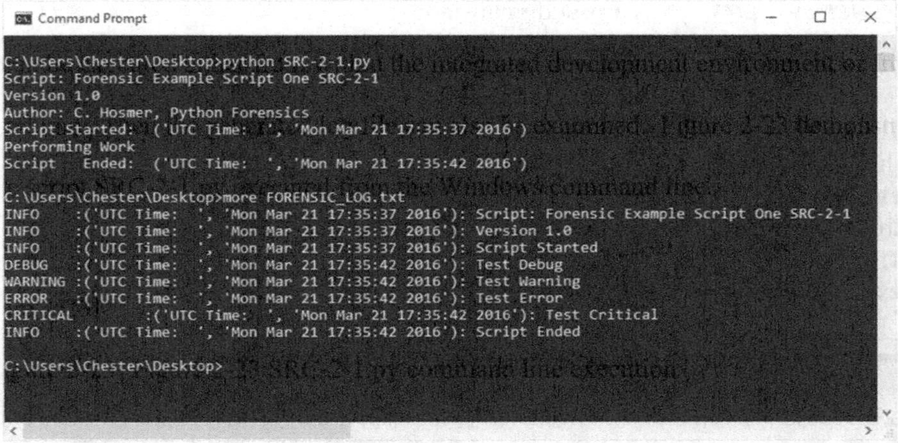

FIG. 2.23 SRC-2-1.py command line execution.

BASIC FORENSIC SCRIPT SRC-2-2.PY

This next script leverages key built-in Python capabilities to address common needs when examining simple files. The script is designed to be cross platform (Windows, MAC, and Linux) without modification. The script purposely only leverages core Python capabilities from the Python Standard Library.

Script SRC-2-2.py

```
'''
Copyright (c) 2016 Chet Hosmer

Permission is hereby granted, free of charge, to any person obtaining a copy
of this software and associated documentation files (the "Software"), to deal
in the Software without restriction, including without limitation the rights
to use, copy, modify, merge, publish, distribute, sublicense, and/or sell
copies of the Software, and to permit persons to whom the Software is
furnished to do so, subject to the following conditions:

The above copyright notice and this permission notice shall be included in
all copies or substantial portions of the Software.

Script Purpose: Forensic File Processing, Hashing and Basic Metadata
extraction

Script Version: 1.0
Script Author:  C.Hosmer

Script Revision History:
Version 1.0 March 2016

'''
```

A

B

```python
# Script Module Importing

# Python Standard Library Modules
import os              # Operating/Filesystem Module
import time            # Basic Time Module
import logging         # Script Logging
import hashlib         # Cryptographic Hashing
import argparse        # Command Line Processing Module


# Import 3rd Party Modules


# End of Script Module Importing
```

C

```python
# Script Constants

'''
Python does not support constants directly
however, by initializing variables here and
specifying them as UPPER_CASE you can make your
intent known
'''
# General Constants
SCRIPT_NAME    = "Script: Forensic Script Two SRC-2-2.py"
SCRIPT_VERSION = "Version 1.0"
SCRIPT_AUTHOR  = "Author: C. Hosmer, Python Forensics"
SCRIPT_LOG     = "./FORENSIC_LOG.txt"

# LOG Constants used as input to LogEvent Function
LOG_DEBUG = 0              # Debugging Event
LOG_INFO  = 1              # Information Event
LOG_WARN  = 2              # Warning Event
LOG_ERR   = 3              # Error Event
LOG_CRIT  = 4              # Critical Event
LOG_OVERWRITE = True       # Set this contstant to True if thE
                           # SCRIPT_LOG
                           # should be overwritten, False if not

# End of Script Constants
```

D

```
# Initialize the Forensic Log

try:
    # If LOG should be overwritten before
    # each run, the remove the old log
    if LOG_OVERWRITE:
        # Verify that the log exists before removing
        if os.path.exists(SCRIPT_LOG):
            os.remove(SCRIPT_LOG)

    # Initialize the Log include the Level and message
    logging.basicConfig(filename=SCRIPT_LOG,
format='%(levelname)s\t:%(message)s', level=logging.DEBUG)

except:
    print "Failed to initialize Logging"
    quit()

# End of Forensic Log Initialization
```

E

```
# Script Functions
'''
If you script will contain functions then insert them
here, before the execution of the main script.  This
will ensure that the functions will be callable from
anywhere in your script
'''

# Function: GetTime()
#
# Returns a string containing the current time
#
# Script will use the local system clock, time, date and
# timezone to calcuate the current time.  sync your system
# clock before using this script
#
# Input: timeStyle = 'UTC', 'LOCAL', default to
#                    UTC Time if you pass in nothing.

def GetTime(timeStyle = "UTC"):

    if timeStyle == 'UTC':
        return ('UTC Time:', time.asctime(time.gmtime(time.time())))
    else:
        return ('Loc Time:',time.asctime(time.localtime(time.time())))

# End GetTime Function ==============================
```

```
# Function: LogEvent()
#
# Logs the event message and specified type
# Input:
#         eventType: LOG_INFO, LOG_WARN, LOG_ERR, LOG_CRIT or LOG_DEBUG
#         eventMessage : string containing the message to be logged


def LogEvent(eventType, eventMessage):

    if type(eventMessage) == str:
        try:

            timeStr = GetTime('UTC')
            # Combine current Time with the eventMessage
            # You can specify either 'UTC' or 'LOCAL'
            # Based on the GetTime parameter

            eventMessage = str(timeStr)+": "+eventMessage

            if eventType == LOG_INFO:
                logging.info(eventMessage)

            elif eventType == LOG_DEBUG:
                logging.debug(eventMessage)

            elif eventType == LOG_WARN:
                logging.warning(eventMessage)

            elif eventType == LOG_ERR:
                logging.error(eventMessage)

            elif eventType == LOG_CRIT:
                logging.critical(eventMessage)

            else:
                logging.info(eventMessage)
        except:
            print "Event Logging Failed"
    else:
        logging.warn('Received invalid event message')


# End LogEvent Function ==========================
```

F

G

```
#
# Name: ParseCommandLine() Function
#
# Process and Validate the command line arguments
# using the Python Standard Library module argparse
#
# Input: none
#
# Return: validated filePath and hashType
#         or generate a detailed error

def ParseCommandLine():

    parser = argparse.ArgumentParser(SCRIPT_NAME)
    parser.add_argument('-p', '--scanPath', type= ValPath, required=True,
help="specifies the file path to scan")
    parser.add_argument('-t', '--hashType', type= ValHash, required=True,
help="enter hashType MD5, SHA1, SH224, SHA256, SHA384 or SHA512")

    theArgs = parser.parse_args()

    return theArgs.scanPath, theArgs.hashType


# End ParseCommandLine =============================
```

H

```
#
# Name: ValPath Function
#
# Function validates validate a directory path
# exists and readable.  Used for argument validation only
#
# Input: a directory path string
#
# Returns the validated directory
# or raises command line errors
#

def ValPath(thePath):

    # Validate the path is a directory
    if not os.path.isdir(thePath):
        raise argparse.ArgumentTypeError('Path does not exist')

    # Validate the path is readable
    if os.access(thePath, os.R_OK):
        return thePath
    else:
        raise argparse.ArgumentTypeError('Path is not readable')

    #End ValidateDirectory =====================================
```

```
#
# Name: ValHash Type Function
#
# Function validates the entered hash string
#
# Input: HashType
#
# Returns the validated hashType upper case
# or raises command line errors
#

def ValHash(theAlg):

    theAlg = theAlg.upper()
    if theAlg in ['MD5', 'SHA1', 'SHA224', 'SHA256', 'SHA384', 'SHA512']:
        return theAlg
    else:
        raise argparse.ArgumentTypeError('Invalid Hash Type Specified')

#End ValHash ================================

# End of Script Functions
```

I

```
# Script Classes

# Class: FileExaminer Class
#
# Desc: Handles basic File Based Examination
# Methods   constructor:   Initializes the Forensic File Object
#                          and Collects Basic Attributes
#                          File Size
#                          MAC Times
#                          Reads file into a buffer
#          hashFile:       Generates the selected one-way hash
#                          of the file
#          destructor:     Deletes the Forensic File Object

class FileExaminer:

    # Constructor

    def __init__(self, theFile):

        #Attributes of the Object

        self.lastError  = "OK"

        # Modified Access Create Time
        self.mactimes  = ["","",""]

        filename, self.fileExtension = os.path.splitext(theFile)

        # File Status Data
        self.mode       = 0
        self.fileSize   = 0
        self.fileType   = "unknown"
        self.uid        = 0
        self.gid        = 0
        self.mountPoint = False
        self.fileRead   = False

        # Possible Hashes
        self.md5        = ""
        self.sha1       = ""
        self.sha224     = ""
        self.sha256     = ""
        self.sha384     = ""
        self.sha512     = ""

        self.lastHash   = ""

        try:

            if os.path.exists(theFile):

                # get the file statistics
                theFileStat =  os.stat(theFile)

                # get the MAC Times and store them in a list
```

J

```
                  self.macTimes = []
                  self.macTimes.append(time.ctime(theFileStat.st_mtime))
                  self.macTimes.append(time.ctime(theFileStat.st_atime))
                  self.macTimes.append(time.ctime(theFileStat.st_ctime))
                  self.mode = theFileStat.st_mode

                  # get and store the File size

                  self.fileSize = theFileStat.st_size

                  # Get and store the ownership information

                  self.uid = theFileStat.st_uid
                  self.gid = theFileStat.st_gid

                  if os.path.isfile(theFile):
                      self.fileType = "File"
                  # Is this a real file?
                  elif os.path.islink(theFile):
                      self.fileType = "Link"
                  # Is This filename actually a directory?
                  elif os.path.isdir(theFile):
                      self.fileType = "Directory"
                  else:
                      self.fileType = "Unknown"

                  # Is the pathname a mount point?
                  if os.path.ismount(theFile):

                      self.mountPoint = True
                  else:
                      self.mountPoint = False

                  # Is the file Accessible for Read?

                  if os.access(theFile, os.R_OK) and self.fileType == "File":

                      # Open the file
                      fp = open(theFile, 'rb')

                      # Assume we have enough space
                      self.buffer = fp.read()

                      # Close the file we have the entire file in memory
                      fp.close()

                      self.fileRead = Trrue
                  else:
                      self.fileRead = False
              else:
                  self.lastError = "File does not exist"
          except:
              self.lastError = "File Exception Raised"
              LogEvent(LOG_ERR,"Examiner-Failed to Process File:"+ theFile)
```

```
# Hash file method
def hashFile(self,hashType):
    try:
        if hashType == "MD5":
            hashObj = hashlib.md5()
            hashObj.update(self.buffer)
            self.lastHash = hashObj.hexdigest().upper()
            self.md5 = self.lastHash
            self.lastHash
            self.lastError = "OK"
            return True
        elif hashType == "SHA1":
            hashObj = hashlib.sha1()
            hashObj.update(self.buffer)
            self.lastHash = hashObj.hexdigest().upper()
            self.sha1 = self.lastHash
            self.lastError = "OK"
            return True
        if hashType == "SHA224":
            hashObj = hashlib.sha224()
            hashObj.update(self.buffer)
            self.lastHash = hashObj.hexdigest().upper()
            self.sha224 = self.lastHash
            self.lastError = "OK"
            return True
        elif hashType == "SHA256":
            hashObj = hashlib.sha256()
            hashObj.update(self.buffer)
            self.lastHash = hashObj.hexdigest().upper()
            self.sha256 = self.lastHash
            self.lastError = "OK"
            return True
        if hashType == "SHA384":
            hashObj = hashlib.sha384()
            hashObj.update(self.buffer)
            self.lastHash = hashObj.hexdigest().upper()
            self.sha384 = self.lastHash
            self.lastError = "OK"
            return True
        elif hashType == "SHA512":
            hashObj = hashlib.sha512()
            hashObj.update(self.buffer)
            self.lastHash = hashObj.hexdigest().upper()
            self.sha512 = self.lastHash
            self.lastError = "OK"
            return True
        else:
            self.lastError = "Invalid Hash Type Specified"
            return False
    except:
        self.lastError = "File Hash Failure"
        LogEvent(LOG_ERR, "File Hashing - Failed to Hash File")
        return False
def __del__(self):
    print
    # End Forensic File Class =====================================
    # End of Script Classes
```

J

```python
# Main Script Starts Here

#
# Script Overview
#
# The purpose of this script it to provide an example
# script that demonstrate and leverage key capabilities
# of Python that provides direct value to the
# forensic investigator.

# This script will perform the following:
#
# 1) Process the command line and obtain the filePath and hashType
# 2) The file names will be stored in a Python List object
# 3) for each file encountered meta-data will be extracted
#     and each file will be hashed with the selected algorithm.
#     the results will be written to the log file.

LogEvent(LOG_INFO, SCRIPT_NAME)
LogEvent(LOG_INFO, SCRIPT_VERSION)
LogEvent(LOG_INFO, "Script Started")

# Print Basic Script Information

print SCRIPT_NAME
print SCRIPT_VERSION
print SCRIPT_AUTHOR

utcTime = GetTime()
print "Script Started: ", utcTime
print

#
# STEP One:
# Parse the Command Line Arguments
#

thePath, theAlg = ParseCommandLine()

print "Path Selected: ", thePath
LogEvent(LOG_INFO, "Path Selected: "+thePath)

print "Algorithm Selected:", theAlg
LogEvent(LOG_INFO,"Algorithm Selected: "+ theAlg)

#
# Step Two extract a list of filenames
# from the path specified
#

listOfFiles = os.listdir(thePath)
```

K

```
#
# Step Three Extract the basic metadata and
#       specified file hash of the each file
#       using the FileExaminer Class
#

for eachFile in listOfFiles:

    # Utilize a try except loop in case encounter
    # Errors during file processing

    try:
        # join the path and file name
        fullPath = os.path.join(thePath, eachFile)

        # create a file examiner object
        feObj = FileExaminer(fullPath)

        # generate the specified hash
        feObj.hashFile(theAlg)

        LogEvent(LOG_INFO, "=============================================")
        LogEvent(LOG_INFO, "File Processed: "+ fullPath)
        LogEvent(LOG_INFO, "File Extension: "+ feObj.fileExtension)
        LogEvent(LOG_INFO, "File Modified:  "+ feObj.macTimes[0])
        LogEvent(LOG_INFO, "File Accessed:  "+ feObj.macTimes[1])
        LogEvent(LOG_INFO, "File Created:   "+ feObj.macTimes[2])
        LogEvent(LOG_INFO, "File Size:      "+ str(feObj.fileSize))
        LogEvent(LOG_INFO, "File Hash:      "+ theAlg + ":" + feObj.lastHash)
        LogEvent(LOG_INFO, "File Owner:     "+ str(feObj.uid))
        LogEvent(LOG_INFO, "File Group:     "+ str(feObj.gid))
        LogEvent(LOG_INFO, "File Mode:      "+ bin(feObj.mode))

        print "===================================================="
        print "File Processed: ", fullPath
        print "File    Ext: ", feObj.fileExtension
        print "MAC   Times: ", feObj.macTimes
        print "File  Size: ", feObj.fileSize
        print "File  Hash: ", theAlg, feObj.lastHash
        print "File Owner: ", feObj.uid
        print "File Group: ", feObj.gid
        print "File Mode:  ", bin(feObj.mode)
        print
    except:
        print "File Processing Error: ", fullPath
        LogEvent(LOG_INFO, "File Processing Error: "+ fullPath)

print
print "Files Processing Completed"

LogEvent(LOG_INFO, "Script End")

utcTime = GetTime('UTC')
print "Script    Ended: ", utcTime


# End of Script Main
```

A Copyright message. No change from the first script.

B The section was updated with two new Python Standard Library modules. First is *hashlib*. The *hashlib* module provides access to cryptographic hash functions including MD5, SHA-1, SHA-256, SHA-512 along with several other variants. The argparse module was also added to the second script. Integrating Python modules with leading forensic platforms typically requires command line argument parsing. This module automates the parsing, collection, and validation of command line arguments.

C The only update to the constants section from the first script is the new *SCRIPT_NAME, "Script: Forensic Script Two SRC-2-2.py."*

D No changes were made to the Forensic Log initialization.

E + F No changes were made to the GetTime() or LogEvent() functions contained with the function definition section.

G The first new function added is the ParseCommandLine function. This function and support modules H and I make up the needed components to process the command line. The ParseCommandLine function leverages the argparse module imported for this script. The argparse module has significant capabilities that go beyond the scope of this description. However, the basic setup is the same. The ParseCommandLine function only contains a few lines of code as shown here.

First, the argparse object is established, and the name of script is provided. When help is requested on the command line, this is the name that is presented.

parser = argparse.ArgumentParser(SCRIPT_NAME)

Next, each possible option is declared using the *add_argument* method. This starts with the option switch, for example, *-p* specifies the directory that will be scanned in this script. The *type* parameter allows for the specification of a validation function to be called to verify the parameter that is being passed. In this case, the name of the function to provide validation is *ValPath*. If the validation function is developed properly, it can ensure that the main program will only receive valid arguments (see Sections H and I for examples). Next, the *required* parameter is set in this case to *True* defining that the user must supply this argument. If they don't, the argument parser will automatically provide an error to the user and the script will abort. Finally, the *help* argument is provided which will provide information to the user under either an error condition or if they specify the embedded *-h* or for the help argument.

```
parser.add_argument('-p', '-scanPath',
                type= ValPath,
                required=True,
                help="specifies the file path to scan")
```

The second argument that is defined is *hashType*. This allows the user to specify which hash algorithm should be used when hashing the file. This argument defines *-t* as the option identifier, *ValHash* as the validation function, the argument is required, and the *help* message specifies the valid entries.

```
parser.add_argument('-t', '-hashType',
                type= ValHash,
                required=True,
                help="enter hashType MD5, SHA1, SH224,
                SHA256, SHA384 or SHA512")
```

Once all the argument requirements are specified, the *parse_args()* method attempts to parse the command line invoking the validation functions for each argument.

```
theArgs = parser.parse_args()
```

If the validation command line arguments are correct (all required arguments are present and valid), the variable *theArgs* contains each of the arguments supplied on the command line. All that is left is to return the valid arguments to the caller (typically the main code section). One of the interesting features of Python is the ability to return multiple values to the caller. This prevents messy pointer and data structure passing in other languages. Therefore, in this case, the function simply returns both the validated *scanPath* and *hashType* to the caller.

```
return theArgs.scanPath, theArgs.hashType
```

Next, let's take a look at the two validation functions *ValPath* and *ValHash*.

H The *ValPath* function is a supporting function for the *ParseCommand-Line*, and, more specifically, the *parse_args()* method of the *argparse* module. In this case, the function needs to validate the directory path provided by the user. As mentioned earlier, if this script was invoked by EnCase, an EnScript, FTK, or some other forensic platform, this would provide validation as well. As you can see in the script, the *ValPath* function performs two separate validations. First, it verifies that the path provided is in fact a valid directory path. This is done using the *os.path.isdir()* method from the miscellaneous operating system Python Standard Library module. If the command line argument is not a valid directory path, the *ValPath* function will raise an exception indicating the error. If the path does exist and is a directory, the second validation is performed to ensure that our script has rights to read from the specified directory. If this test passes, then the function returns the valid path; otherwise, it will raise the appropriate exception.

I The second validation function *ValHash* is much simpler, and it reveals a nice feature of the Python language. Since the set of legal strings are known MD5, SHA1..., we can validate that the string passed to the function is contained in the *List* of legal values, essentially with a single line of Python code: Reading this line of code like English: Are the contents of the "theAlg" contained in the list of possible values?

```
if theAlg in ['MD5', 'SHA1', 'SHA224', 'SHA256', 'SHA384', 'SHA512']:
```

if the answer is yes, then the string is validated; otherwise, the function raises the appropriate error. Also, to simplify the list search, the *upper()* method is used to change all the characters from the command line entry to upper case before the check is performed.

J This code section represents a class, specifically the *FileExaminer* class. This class, once instantiated, is no different than using a string in Python as everything is a class. Classes have attributes and methods relating to the object that it becomes. In this case, the object encompasses a single file and performs a set of operations to examine the contents of the file. The class can be extended (this will be done later in the book) to perform even deeper analysis of files. To keep things simple, when the object is first activated, it automatically extracts some details about the file that it encompasses. For example, it determines and stores attributes such as the size of the file, last modified, and last accessed and created dates/time (MAC Times for short), determines the group and user id, and reads the contents of the file. The object also provides a method to hash the file using various hashing algorithms provided by the Python Standard Library hashlib. The specific method supplied by the object is *HashFile()*.

J The final section for this script is the main section of code. Based on the setup of various functions, the main script section mainly orchestrates the activity, prints out messages, and saves results to the Forensic Log. More specifically, this main program performs three basic actions:

(1) Utilizes the *ParseCommandLine()* function to obtain the command line arguments.

(2) Obtains the list of files that are contained in the directory specified by the scanPath. Note this Python list is created in one line of code by using the *os.listdir()* method.

(3) Finally, the script processes each file in the list creating a *FileExaminer* object. Then, based on the *hashType* specified on the command line, the script generates the specified hash value. The rest of the script prints out and saves the attributes and hash value to the log file.

Executing SRC-2-2.py

Executing SRC-2-2.py from the command line can be accomplished as follows:

First, the script is executed with only the -h option to reveal the required command line arguments.

```
C:\Users\Chester\Desktop>python SRC-2-2.py -h
Script: Forensic Script Two SRC-2-2.py
Version 1.0
Author: C. Hosmer, Python Forensics
Script Started: ('UTC Time: ', 'Tue Mar 22 02:25:29 2016')
usage: Script: Forensic Script Two SRC-2-2.py [-h] -p SCANPATH -t HASHTYPE
optional arguments:
  -h, -help              show this help message and exit
  -p SCANPATH, -scanPath SCANPATH
                         specifies the file path to scan
  -t HASHTYPE, -hashType HASHTYPE
                         enter hashType MD5, SHA1, SH224, SHA256, SHA384 or
                         SHA512
```

Subsequently, the script is executed using the required command line arguments. In this case, the path and hash type is specified.

```
C:\Users\Chester\Desktop>python SRC-2-2.py -p ./images -t md5

Script: Forensic Script Two SRC-2-2.py
Version 1.0
Author: C. Hosmer, Python Forensics
Script Started: ('UTC Time: ', 'Tue Mar 22 02:26:12 2016')
Path Selected: ./images
Algorithm Selected: MD5
===================================================
File Processed: ./images\Biking.jpg
File  Ext:     .jpg
MAC Times:     ['Thu Mar 10 11:23:38 2016', 'Mon Mar 21 22:25:36 2016', 'Mon
Mar 21 22:25:36 2016']
File  Size:    624744
File  Hash:    MD5 4335A72251DFD42E301A0315FA1AA15B
File Owner:    0
File Group:    0
File Mode:     0b1000000110110110

===================================================
File Processed: ./images\Castle.JPG
File  Ext:    .JPG
```

```
MAC Times:   ['Thu Mar 10 11:23:38 2016', 'Mon Mar 21 22:25:36 2016', 'Mon Mar
21 22:25:36 2016']
File  Size:  1224201
File  Hash:  MD5 0A23F62DC9ED694CA80E3CA97F2D8996
File Owner:  0
File Group:  0
File Mode:  0b1000000110110110

=====================================================
File Processed: ./images\Cat.jpg
File  Ext:  .jpg
MAC Times:   ['Thu Mar 10 11:23:38 2016', 'Mon Mar 21 22:25:36 2016', 'Mon Mar
21 22:25:36 2016']
File  Size:  446759
File  Hash:  MD5 1894912F5030242D93E45E370F5D3BD5
File Owner:  0
File Group:  0
File Mode:  0b1000000110110110

=====================================================
File Processed: ./images\Deutchland.JPG
File  Ext:  .JPG
MAC Times:   ['Thu Mar 10 11:23:38 2016', 'Mon Mar 21 22:25:36 2016', 'Mon Mar
21 22:25:36 2016']
File  Size:  600630
File  Hash:  MD5 F34A9506E92C83F94170232926564F11
File Owner: 0
File Group: 0
File Mode:  0b1000000110110110

=====================================================
File Processed: ./images\Disney.jpg
File  Ext:  .jpg
MAC Times:   ['Thu Mar 10 11:23:38 2016', 'Mon Mar 21 22:25:36 2016', 'Mon Mar
21 22:25:36 2016']
File  Size:  304930
File  Hash:  MD5 732A289B7DD8C7DD28D4D73ED2480BCF
File Owner:  0
File Group:  0
File Mode:  0b1000000110110110

=====================================================
File Processed: ./images\dscn0011.jpg
File  Ext:  .jpg
```

```
MAC Times:  ['Thu Mar 10 11:23:38 2016', 'Mon Mar 21 22:25:36 2016', 'Mon Mar
21 22:25:36 2016']
File  Size: 96831
File  Hash: MD5 B0E335DE41D1CF5ADF6DFE0A8F7E3B88
File Owner: 0
File Group: 0
File Mode: 0b1000000110110110


==================================================
File Processed: ./images\kinderscout.jpg
File  Ext:  .jpg
MAC Times:  ['Thu Mar 10 11:23:38 2016', 'Mon Mar 21 22:25:36 2016', 'Mon Mar
21 22:25:36 2016']
File  Size: 98012
File  Hash: MD5 C3681F1A5A50BDEC9F5B00018CA71F66
File Owner: 0
File Group: 0
File Mode: 0b1000000110110110


==================================================
File Processed: ./images\Munich.JPG
File  Ext:  .JPG
MAC Times:  ['Thu Mar 10 11:23:38 2016', 'Mon Mar 21 22:25:36 2016', 'Mon Mar
21 22:25:36 2016']
File  Size: 252607
File  Hash: MD5 B1D4082F26F52F3EB54AF98F8EE10345
File Owner: 0
File Group: 0
File Mode: 0b1000000110110110


==================================================
File Processed: ./images\Rome.jpg
File  Ext:  .jpg
MAC Times:  ['Thu Mar 10 11:23:38 2016', 'Mon Mar 21 22:25:36 2016', 'Mon Mar
21 22:25:36 2016']
File  Size: 3352190
File  Hash: MD5 D0D7EFC9091CE701271146F31F61271E
File Owner: 0
File Group: 0
File Mode: 0b1000000110110110
```

```
===================================================
File Processed: ./images\Turtle.jpg
File  Ext:  .jpg
MAC Times:  ['Thu Mar 10 11:23:38 2016', 'Mon Mar 21 22:25:36 2016', 'Mon Mar
21 22:25:36 2016']
File  Size: 91329
File  Hash: MD5 031113080810C1A8345C68237BD88549
File Owner: 0
File Group: 0
File Mode: 0b1000000110110110

===================================================
File Processed: ./images\zzz.jpg
File  Ext:  .jpg
MAC Times:  ['Thu Mar 10 11:23:38 2016', 'Mon Mar 21 22:25:36 2016', 'Mon Mar
21 22:25:36 2016']
File  Size: 5459
File  Hash: MD5 40374D33463DFE213D31CCB0E1DEDC22
File Owner: 0
File Group: 0
File Mode: 0b1000000110110110

Files Processing Completed
Script  Ended: ('UTC Time: ', 'Tue Mar 22 02:26:12 2016')
```

Finally, examining a segment of the FORENSIC_LOG.TXT file reveals the following.

```
C:\Users\Chester\Desktop>more FORENSIC_LOG.txt
INFO   :('UTC Time: ', 'Tue Mar 22 02:32:04 2016'): Script: Forensic Script Two SRC-2-2.py
INFO   :('UTC Time: ', 'Tue Mar 22 02:32:04 2016'): Version 1.0
INFO   :('UTC Time: ', 'Tue Mar 22 02:32:04 2016'): Script Started
INFO   :('UTC Time: ', 'Tue Mar 22 02:32:04 2016'): Path Selected:  ./images
INFO   :('UTC Time: ', 'Tue Mar 22 02:32:04 2016'): Algorithm Selected: MD5
INFO   :('UTC Time: ', 'Tue Mar 22 02:32:04 2016'): =============================
INFO   :('UTC Time: ', 'Tue Mar 22 02:32:04 2016'): File Processed:  ./images\Biking.jpg
INFO   :('UTC Time: ', 'Tue Mar 22 02:32:04 2016'): File Extension: .jpg
INFO   :('UTC Time: ', 'Tue Mar 22 02:32:04 2016'): File Modified: Thu Mar 10 11:23:38 2016
INFO   :('UTC Time: ', 'Tue Mar 22 02:32:04 2016'): File Accessed: Mon Mar 21 22:25:36 2016
INFO   :('UTC Time: ', 'Tue Mar 22 02:32:04 2016'): File Created:   Mon Mar 21 22:25:36 2016
INFO   :('UTC Time: ', 'Tue Mar 22 02:32:04 2016'): File Size:     624744
INFO   :('UTC Time: ', 'Tue Mar 22 02:32:04 2016'): File Hash:
MD5:4335A72251DFD42E301A0315FA1AA15B
INFO   :('UTC Time: ', 'Tue Mar 22 02:32:04 2016'): File Owner:    0
INFO   :('UTC Time: ', 'Tue Mar 22 02:32:04 2016'): File Group:    0
INFO   :('UTC Time: ', 'Tue Mar 22 02:32:04 2016'): File Mode:     0b100000011011010
INFO   :('UTC Time: ', 'Tue Mar 22 02:32:04 2016'): =============================
INFO   :('UTC Time: ', 'Tue Mar 22 02:32:04 2016'): File Processed: ./images\Castle.JPG
INFO   :('UTC Time: ', 'Tue Mar 22 02:32:04 2016'): File Extension: .JPG
INFO   :('UTC Time: ', 'Tue Mar 22 02:32:04 2016'): File Modified: Thu Mar 10 11:23:38 2016
INFO   :('UTC Time: ', 'Tue Mar 22 02:32:04 2016'): File Accessed: Mon Mar 21 22:25:36 2016
INFO   :('UTC Time: ', 'Tue Mar 22 02:32:04 2016'): File Created:   Mon Mar 21 22:25:36 2016
INFO   :('UTC Time: ', 'Tue Mar 22 02:32:04 2016'): File Size:     1224201
INFO   :('UTC Time: ', 'Tue Mar 22 02:32:04 2016'): File Hash:
MD5:0A23F62DC9ED694CA80B3CA97F2D8996
INFO   :('UTC Time: ', 'Tue Mar 22 02:32:04 2016'): File Owner:    0
INFO   :('UTC Time: ', 'Tue Mar 22 02:32:04 2016'): File Group:    0
INFO   :('UTC Time: ', 'Tue Mar 22 02:32:04 2016'): File Mode:     0b100000011011010
INFO   :('UTC Time: ', 'Tue Mar 22 02:32:04 2016'): =============================
INFO   :('UTC Time: ', 'Tue Mar 22 02:32:04 2016'): File Processed: ./images\Cat.jpg
INFO   :('UTC Time: ', 'Tue Mar 22 02:32:04 2016'): File Extension: .jpg
INFO   :('UTC Time: ', 'Tue Mar 22 02:32:04 2016'): File Modified: Thu Mar 10 11:23:38 2016
- More (24%) -
```

Next Steps

This should provide a good example of the basic Python language constructs, including use of built-in data types, defining functions, creating and using classes/objects, interface with the underlying file system, and providing a template that can be adapted. The most important thing in learning to adapt Python to your specific forensic application is by doing it. Thus, take these examples/template and load them into your favorite Integrated Development Environment and take them for a test drive and then add your own enhancements and ideas. All the source files for this book are available free to those purchasing the book. Details on obtaining the source code examples are included upfront in the preface section.

REVIEW

This chapter first provided a walk-through of installing Python and a suitable Integrated Development Environment, WingIDE. Next, we created a template Forensic Script that can be reused when creating new simple or expanded scripts. We extended the template, by leveraging and exposing useful Python Language elements and Python Standard Library modules to process a set of files. Finally, we introduced the *FileExaminer ()* Class to extract meaningful information from provided files.

CHALLENGE PROBLEMS

(1) One obvious enhancement to the script is to process the specified directory and associated subdirectories. Hint, use the *os.walk ()* method to walk the directory tree from the starting point provided.
(2) Storing the results in the forensic log and on screen is a good start. The next step is to write the output to a comma separated value (CSV) file, or an XML document … or maybe create a SQLite database. Hint, the Python Standard Library includes: *csv*, *xml*, *json*, and *sqlite3* that make integration with these common formats easy as py.
(3) Finally, define several enhancements to the *FileExaminer* Class that would dig deeper into the contents of certain file types (i.e., images, document, or multimedia files).

Additional Resources

Hosmer C. Python forensics: a workbench for inventing and sharing digital forensic technology. Waltham, MA: Syngress; 2014. ISBN: 978-0124186767.

Python Standard Library, https://docs.python.org/2/library/index.html.

## CHAPTER 3

Integrating Python With MPE+

INTRODUCTION

Mobile Phone Examiner Plus (MPE+) is a stand-alone mobile device investigation solution that includes extensive smart device acquisition and analysis capabilities from AccessData. With a different approach to digital mobile forensics, MPE+ allows mobile forensic examiners to expand on the built-in capabilities of MPE+ by adding custom Python scripts to the equation. This custom scripts leverage the built-in pythonScripter application directly integrated with MPE+. This chapter assumes that users have access to MPE+ and are familiar with the basic function.

MPE+ Basics

Once MPE+ is installed, the application is launched as shown in Fig. 3.1. More information regarding MPE+ is available directly from AccessData at www. accessdata.com.

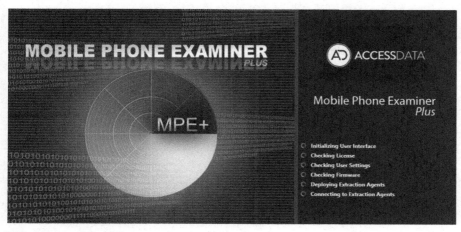

FIG. 3.1 Launching MPE+.

Integrating Python with Leading Computer Forensics Platforms. http://dx.doi.org/10.1016/B978-0-12-809949-0.00003-0

Once launched, the MPE+ home screen shown in Fig. 3.2 is displayed. The user will most commonly select the "Import Image" function from the main tool bar as shown in Fig. 3.3. This brings up a dialog box for the selection of a previously acquired image as shown in Fig. 3.4.

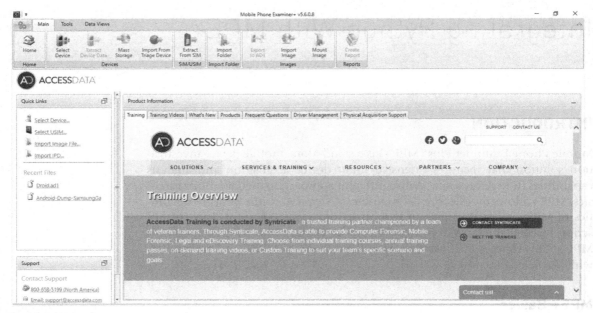

FIG. 3.2 MPE+ home screen.

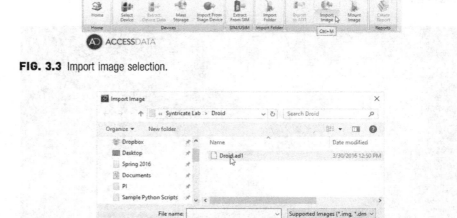

FIG. 3.3 Import image selection.

FIG. 3.4 MPE+ select phone image for import.

Once the image is selected, MPE+ will initialize the image as shown in Fig. 3.5 and process the image by extracting and categorizing key elements. Once the image is populated, we are most interested in the extract file content. The main toolbar provides an option for selecting and displaying the extracted filesystem (Fig. 3.6).

FIG. 3.5 Initializing MPE+ image.

FIG. 3.6 Selecting files for review in MPE+.

Selecting "files" reveals the Filesystem panel shown in Fig. 3.7. This provides tree control navigation to all related content.

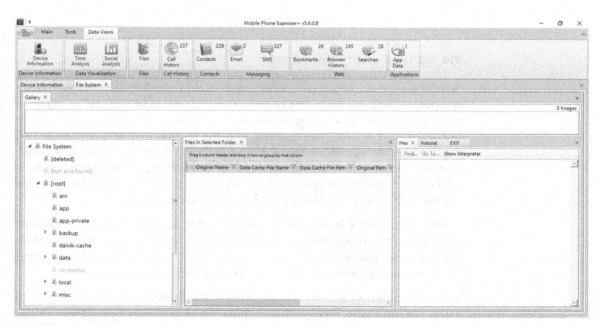

FIG. 3.7 MPE+ file system panel.

Launching the pythonScripter

Selecting any object in the Filesystem panel (folders or individual files) and then right clicking reveal an option drop down. This drop down includes the "Run pythonScripter" option as shown in Fig. 3.8.

FIG. 3.8 Launching MPE+ Python scripter.

Selecting a specific object (file, folder, or even the complete filesystem) creates a temporary work environment keeping the evidence held with MPE+ separate from any Python processing of the selected objects. All the selected content is copied to this new environment, and the pythonScripter application will be launched as shown in Fig. 3.9. The pythonScripter application is a full-featured Python 3.5.× environment (as of this writing). AccessData regularly updates the environment to the latest Python version. For more information on the pythonScripter, please refer the MPE+ Users Manual.

Once pythonScript is launched, you can select a Python script to execute. PythonScripter comes with several file and folder scripts that are available from the pull down menu labeled "preset scripts." These scripts provide useful scripts for processing various folders or file data from extracted images.

The second option that we will be using is the Browse option allowing us to select custom Python scripts that we have developed. Selecting Browse brings up a simple navigation browser where we can locate the scripts we wish to execute. Fig. 3.10 shows our first script which is **PF_MPE_PARAMETERS.py**. It should be noted this script provides a simple integration with MPE + in order to demonstrate the integration method. Selecting this script loads it into the script window and readies it for execution as shown in Fig. 3.11 labeled A. In addition, you can see the "evidence path" Labeled B. This is where the files, folders, or complete filesystem (depending upon what was selected) were copied from MPE + for processing.

FIG. 3.9 MPE + pythonScripter main screen.

FIG. 3.10 Browse to desired script.

Connecting the Dots ... MPE+ with Python

The interface between MPE + and the selected Python script is very straight-forward, which provides great flexibility and simplicity when developing Python scripts. The interface is based upon argument passing when launching the application. The concept of passing command line arguments to applications dates back almost 30 years and uses something called the argument vector (or simply argv). As an example, when processing a command line such as the following:

FIG. 3.11 Selected script loaded.

PF_PARAMETERS_MPE.PY C:

The argument vector contains only two elements.

    (0) PF_PARAMETERS_MPE.PY
    (1) C:\

Notice that I labeled them 0 and 1, as the vector or array that holds these values is indexed starting with the first position designated as 0, not 1.

As mentioned above, MPE+ copies the selected file, folder, or complete filesystem to a temporary directory on the local drive. Thus in order for Python to process the files or directories, MPE+ passes the full path to the selected file or directory, along with the temporary name of the Python script. Thus one of the first things we need to obtain is the temporary name of the Python script being executed along with the full path that points to the file or folder to be processed.

Python scripts, like most applications, provide a simple method for obtaining the contents of argv. Only a couple of lines of code are required to do this in Python.

```
from sys import argv        # Import agrv from the system Module
scriptName, scriptPath = argv        # Obtain the two arguments

print(scriptName)
print(scriptPath)
```

Executing this script produces this following output:

```
Script Name: C:\Users\Chester\AppData\Local\MPETEM~1\TEMPPY~1\6B37BC~1.PY
Script Path: C:\Users\Chester\AppData\Local\MPETEM~1\TEMPPY~1\evidence\77DAB1~1\app
```

For this execution, I simply selected a directory using MPE+ (specifically the directory named "app" to be exact) and then executed this simple script. You notice that the script is copied to the temporary folder, and the evidence is copied to a directory below the same temporary folder named ...*evidence \77Dab1~1*. The evidence in this case is in the folder *app* and would include any subfolders contained within *app* on the mobile device.

BUILDING AND MPE+ PYTHON TEMPLATE

As proposed in Chapter 2, the development of a template for each Python integration will provide a fast onramp to developing Python scripts that directly support the integration. I have developed two template scripts for MPE+. The first is **PF_MPE_PARAMETERS.py** and the second is **PF_MPE_BASIC.py**. Both provide a template for integration depending upon your objectives. PF_MPE_BASIC.py adds in the common functions LogEvent, GetTime and also provides a defined main entry point.

PF_MPE_PARAMETERS

```
'''

Copyright (c) 2016 Chet Hosmer

Permission is hereby granted, free of charge, to any person obtaining a copy
of this software and associated documentation files (the "Software"), to deal
in the Software without restriction, including without limitation the rights
to use, copy, modify, merge, publish, distribute, sublicense,
and/or sell copies of the Software, and to permit persons to whom the
Software is furnished to do so, subject to the following conditions:

The above copyright notice and this permission notice shall be included in
all copies or substantial portions of the Software.

Script Purpose: Python Template for MPE+ Integration
Script Version: 1.0
Script Author:  C.Hosmer

Script Revision History:
Version 1.0 April 2016

'''
```

A

B
```
# Script Module Importing

# Python Standard Library Modules

import os                 # Operating/Filesystem Module
from sys import argv      # The systems argument vector, in Python this is
                          # a list of elements from the command line
```

C
```
# Script Constants

'''
Python does not support constants directly
however, by initializing variables here and
specifying them as UPPER_CASE you can make your
intent known
'''
# General Constants
SCRIPT_NAME    = "Script: MPE+ Command Line Arguments"
SCRIPT_VERSION = "Version 1.0"
SCRIPT_AUTHOR  = "Author: C. Hosmer, Python Forensics"
SCRIPT_RELEASE = "April 2016"
```

```
intent known
'''
# General Constants
SCRIPT_NAME    = "Script: MPE+ Command Line Arguments"
SCRIPT_VERSION = "Version 1.0"
SCRIPT_AUTHOR  = "Author: C. Hosmer, Python Forensics"
SCRIPT_RELEASE = "April 2016"
```

D
```
# Print out some basics

print(SCRIPT_NAME)
print(SCRIPT_AUTHOR)
print(SCRIPT_VERSION, SCRIPT_RELEASE)
```

```python
# Obtain the command line arguments using
# the system argument vector

# For MPE+ Scripts the length of the argument vector is
# always 2  scriptName, path

if len(argv) == 2:
    scriptName, path = argv
else:
    print(argv, "Invalid Command line")
    quit()

print("Command Line Argument Vector")
print("Script Name: ", scriptName)
print("Script Path: ", path)
```

E

```python
# Verify the path exists and determine
# the path type

if os.path.exists(path):
    print("Path Exists")
    if os.path.isdir(path):
        print("Path is a directory")
    elif os.path.isfile(path):
        print("Path is a file")
    else:
        print(path, "is invalid")
else:
    print(path, "Does not exist")

print ("Script Complete")
```

F

A This section provides a place for you to include your copyright notice regarding the script. Since Python is intended to be an open source language, I have chosen this copyright notice for all the scripts that I develop. Your situation may differ, and the restrictions for use and distribution may also differ. However, you should clearly define this section if you intend for others to utilize and share your code.

B This section defines Python modules that will be imported into our script. This script only utilizes Python Standard Library modules. The script imports the os module and from the sys module only imports argv.

os: The os module contains miscellaneous operating system interfaces. For example, use this if you wish to determine if a file or path exists, if you wish to navigate the filesystem or obtain the names of files. The module should contain all methods that are useful when examining the file system.

from sys import argv: In Python you are able to import the whole module as with os above, or in this case, only import items from the module that are needed as done here. In this case, we only require the argument vector list (argv) from the system module.

$\boxed{\text{C}}$ The next section defines any pseudo constants that you will be using throughout your script. Python is a loosely typed language and as such, constants are not really constants, since they can be changed within your code, they are typically referred to as pseudo constants. A way to separate the pseudo constants from variables is how you define them. In the case of constants, I use all capital letters and separate words with the underscore character. For example, *SCRIPT_NAME* is a string of characters that is meant to represent the name of the script and should not be changed.

SCRIPT_NAME = "Script: MPE+ Command Line Arguments"

$\boxed{\text{D}}$ The section simply prints out the basic constants that we have defined in Section C. These include the *SCRIPT_NAME*, *SCRIPT_AUTHOR*, *SCRIPT_VERSION*, and *SCRIPT_RELEASE*.

$\boxed{\text{E}}$ In this section, the argument vector count is examined to ensure that it contains exactly two arguments. If this test passes, the arguments script name and path are extracted from argv and stored in the variables *scriptName* and *path*, respectively. The contents of these variables are then printed to the console.

$\boxed{\text{F}}$ This section validates the path extracted from argv. The following tests are performed against the extracted path string. (1) Does the *path* exist; (2) does the *path* point to a directory; and (3) does the *path* point to a file. To accomplish these tests, the Python *os* module methods are leveraged. Specifically:

os.path.exists() Verify the existence of the path
os.path.isdir() Determines if the path is a directory
os.path.isfile() Determines if the path is a file

Note: All the "*is*" related methods return either True or False. During each step of the process, this section prints out the results obtained from the specific "*is*" related methods.

PF_MPE_PARAMETERS

To execute the script, the Execute button is selected as shown in Fig. 3.12. This will execute the loaded script using the command line parameters provided by MPE+. The result of the script execution is shown in Fig. 3.13.

FIG. 3.12 Select execute to run the loaded script.

FIG. 3.13 MPE + Python scripter console results.

In Figs. 3.14 and 3.15, a file vs a directory is selected from within MPE+. The same **PF_MPE_PARAMETERS** script is selected and then executed. As you can see this results in the proper results indicating that path now points to a file instead of a directory.

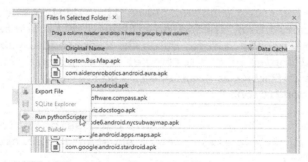

FIG. 3.14 Launch MPE + Python scripter with a selected file.

PF_MPE_BASIC.py

The PF_MPE_BASIC.py script builds upon the PF_MPE_PARAMETERS script to create a more complete template. Only the main section is discussed here as all the other code sections have been covered in PF_MPE_PARAMETERS or in Chapter 2 in the **Script SRC-2-1.py** descriptions.

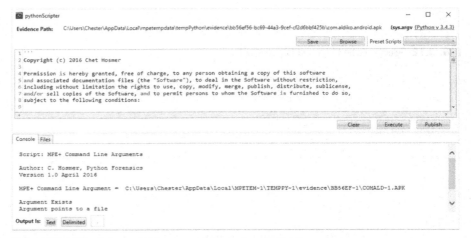

FIG. 3.15 MPE+ Python scripter argument results for selected file.

' ' '

Copyright (c) 2016 Chet Hosmer

Permission is hereby granted, free of charge, to any person obtaining a copy of this software and associated documentation files (the "Software"), to deal in the Software without restriction, including without limitation the rights to use, copy, modify, merge, publish, distribute, sublicense, and/or sell copies of the Software, and to permit persons to whom the Software is furnished to do so, subject to the following conditions:

The above copyright notice and this permission notice shall be included in all copies or substantial portions of the Software.

Script Purpose: Python Template for MPE+ Integration
Script Version: 1.0
Script Author: C.Hosmer

Script Revision History:
Version 1.0 April 2016

```python
'''
# Script Module Importing

# Python Standard Library Modules
import os                    # Operating/Filesystem Module
import time                  # Basic Time Module
import logging               # Script Logging
from sys import argv         # The systems argument vector, in Python this is
                             # a list of elements from the command
line

# Import 3rd Party Modules

# End of Script Module Importing

# Script Constants

'''
Python does not support constants directly
however, by initializing variables here and
specifying them as UPPER_CASE you can make your
intent known
'''
# General Constants
SCRIPT_NAME    = "Script: MPE+ Template"
SCRIPT_VERSION = "Version 1.0"
SCRIPT_AUTHOR  = "Author: C. Hosmer, Python Forensics"
SCRIPT_LOG     = "C:/SYN/BASIC/FORENSIC_LOG.txt"

# LOG Constants used as input to LogEvent Function
LOG_DEBUG = 0              # Debugging Event
LOG_INFO  = 1              # Information Event
LOG_WARN  = 2              # Warning Event
LOG_ERR   = 3              # Error Event
LOG_CRIT  = 4              # Critical Event
LOG_OVERWRITE = True       # Set this contstant to True if the SCRIPT_LOG
                           # should be overwritten, False if not

# End of Script Constants

# Initialize Forensic Logging

try:
    # If LOG should be overwritten before
    # each run, the remove the old log
    if LOG_OVERWRITE:
```

```python
        # Verify that the log exists before removing
        if os.path.exists(SCRIPT_LOG):
            os.remove(SCRIPT_LOG)

    # Initialize the Log include the Level and message
    logging.basicConfig(filename=SCRIPT_LOG,        format='%
(levelname)s\t:%(message)s', level=logging.DEBUG)

except:
    print ("Failed to initialize Logging")
    quit()

# End of Forensic Log Initialization

# Script Functions
'''
If you script will contain functions then insert them
here, before the execution of the main script. This
will ensure that the functions will be callable from
anywhere in your script
'''

# Function: GetTime()
#
# Returns a string containing the current time
#
# Script will use the local system clock, time, date and timezone
# to calcuate the current time. Thus you should sync your system
# clock before using this script
#
# Input: timeStyle = 'UTC', 'LOCAL', the function will default to
#                     UTC Time if you pass in nothing.

def GetTime(timeStyle = "UTC"):

    if timeStyle == 'UTC':
        return ('UTC Time: ', time.asctime(time.gmtime(time.
time())))
    else:
        return ('LOC Time: ', time.asctime(time.localtime
(time.time())))

# End GetTime Function ==============================
```

```python
# Function: LogEvent()
#
# Logs the event message and specified type
# Input:
#        eventType: LOG_INFO, LOG_WARN, LOG_ERR, LOG_CRIT or LOG_DEBUG

#        eventMessage : string containing the message to be logged

def LogEvent(eventType, eventMessage):

    if type(eventMessage) == str:
        try:

            timeStr = GetTime('UTC')
            # Combine current Time with the eventMessage
            # You can specify either 'UTC' or 'LOCAL'
            # Based on the GetTime parameter

            eventMessage = str(timeStr)+": "+eventMessage

            if eventType == LOG_INFO:
                logging.info(eventMessage)

            elif eventType == LOG_DEBUG:
                logging.debug(eventMessage)

            elif eventType == LOG_WARN:
                logging.warning(eventMessage)

            elif eventType == LOG_ERR:
                logging.error(eventMessage)

            elif eventType == LOG_CRIT:
                logging.critical(eventMessage)

            else:
                logging.info(eventMessage)
        except:
            logging.warn("Event messages must be strings")
    else:
        logging.warn('Received invalid event message')

# End LogEvent Function ==========================
```

```
# Main Script Starts Here
#
# Script Overview
#
# The purpose of this script it to provide an example
# script that demonstrate and leverage key capabilities
# of Python that provides direct value to the
# forensic investigator.

        if __name__ == '__main__':

            LogEvent(LOG_INFO, SCRIPT_NAME)
            LogEvent(LOG_INFO, SCRIPT_VERSION)
            LogEvent(LOG_INFO, "Script Started")

            # Print Basic Script Information

            # Parse the Command Line Arguments
            # Try to parse the command line argument provided by MPE+
            # Obtain the command line arguments using
            # the system argument vector

            # For MPE+ Scripts the length of the argument vector is
            # always 2   scriptName, path

            if len(argv) == 2:
                scriptName, path = argv
            else:
                LogEvent(LOG_INFO, argv + " Invalid Command line")
                quit()

            LogEvent(LOG_INFO,"Command Line Argument Vector")
            LogEvent(LOG_INFO,"Script Name: " + scriptName)
            LogEvent(LOG_INFO,"Script Path: " + path)

            # Verify the path exists and determine
            # the path type

            if os.path.exists(path):
                LogEvent(LOG_INFO,"Path Exists")
                if os.path.isdir(path):
                    LogEvent(LOG_INFO,"Path is a directory")
                elif os.path.isfile(path):
                    LogEvent(LOG_INFO,"Path is a file")
                else:
                    LogEvent(LOG_ERR, path + " is invalid")
            else:
                LogEvent(LOG_ERR, path + " Does not exist")

            with open(SCRIPT_LOG, 'r') as logData:
                for eachLine in logData:
                    print(eachLine)
```

M

$\boxed{\text{M}}$ The main section of the MPE+ template differs in a couple import ways. First, instead of printing content to the console throughout the script using the `print()` function, the script instead posts all processing results to the forensic log using the `LogEvent()` function. This provides a consistent method of tracking the script's progress and at the same time creates a forensic log file with timestamps included. Once the script and all the processing elements are completed, it opens the log file and prints the contents of the log to the console. Figs. 3.16–3.18 depict the progression:

FIG. 3.16 Launch MPE+ python scripter with a selected folder.

FIG. 3.17 Browse and select Python script.

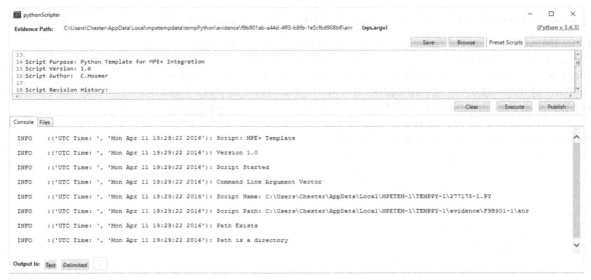

FIG. 3.18 MPE+ Python scripter argument results for selected folder.

Fig. 3.16: Selects a folder to process within MPE+ and launches the pythonScripter

Fig. 3.17: Selects and PF_MPE_BASIC.py script

Fig. 3.18: Executes the PF_MPE_BASIC.py script and depicts the output from the log file, complete with the associated time stamp values

CREATING A HashSearch MPE+ PYTHON SCRIPT

Now that we have created a working MPE+ template, let's put together a useful forensic script that employs the template. For this I have chosen to develop **PF_HashSearch.py**. The basics of the script are as follows:

(1) Provide a list of MD5 hashes to search
(2) Select any folder from with MPE+ to process
(3) Generate an MD5 hash for each file contained in the selected folder including any subfolders
(4) Log the results of each hash operation to the log
(5) Create a comma-separated value (CSV) file for the results
(6) Compare each generated hash with the list of hashes to search
(7) Report any matches to the log file and to the CSV file
(8) Dump the report file to the console when completed, along with a summary of any hash matches
(9) Publish the results back to MPE+

The following PF_HashSearch.py script addresses these requirements while providing a model for future development of MPE+ Python scripts.

```
Script Purpose: Python HashSearch for MPE+
Script Version: 1.0
Script Author: C.Hosmer

Script Revision History:
Version 1.0 April 2016


'''
```

```
        # Script Module Importing

        # Python Standard Library Modules
A       import os                # Operating/Filesystem Module
        import time              # Basic Time Module
        import logging           # Script Logging
        import hashlib           # Python Hashing Module
        from sys import argv     # Command Line arguments

# Import 3rd Party Modules

# End of Script Module Importing


# Script Constants
```

```
'''
Python does not support constants directly
however, by initializing variables here and
specifying them as UPPER_CASE you can make your
intent known
'''
```

```
        # General Constants
        SCRIPT_NAME     = "Script: Hash Search for MPE+ "
        SCRIPT_VERSION  = "Version 1.0"
        SCRIPT_AUTHOR   = "Author: C. Hosmer, Python Forensics"
        SCRIPT_LOG      = "C:/SYN/HashSearch/FORENSIC_LOG.txt"
        SRC_HASH        = "C:/SYN/HashSearch/Hashes.txt"
        CSV             = "C:/SYN/HashSearch/results.csv"
```

```
# LOG Constants used as input to LogEvent Function
LOG_DEBUG = 0              # Debugging Event
LOG_INFO  = 1              # Information Event
LOG_WARN  = 2              # Warning Event
LOG_ERR   = 3              # Error Event
LOG_CRIT  = 4              # Critical Event
LOG_OVERWRITE = True       # Set this contstant to True if the
SCRIPT_LOG
                           # should be overwritten, False if not

# End of Script Constants

# Initialize Forensic Logging

try:
    # If LOG should be overwritten before
    # each run, the remove the old log
    if LOG_OVERWRITE:
        # Verify that the log exists before removing
        if os.path.exists(SCRIPT_LOG):
            os.remove(SCRIPT_LOG)

    # Initialize the Log include the Level and message
    logging.basicConfig(filename=SCRIPT_LOG,
format='%(levelname)s\t:%(message)s', level=logging.DEBUG)

except:
    print ("Failed to initialize Logging")
    quit()

# End of Forensic Log Initialization
```

```
      # Initialize CSV Output File
      # Write Heading Line
      try:
          csvOut = open(CSV, "w")
          csvOut.write("FileName, MD5 Hash, Match, Category \n")
      except:
          print ("Failed to initialize CSV File  .. Make sure file is not open")
          quit()
```

C

```
# Script Functions
'''
If you script will contain functions then insert them
here, before the execution of the main script. This
will ensure that the functions will be callable from
anywhere in your script
'''


# Function: GetTime()
#
# Returns a string containing the current time
#
# Script will use the local system clock, time, date and timezone
# to calcuate the current time. Thus you should sync your system
# clock before using this script
#
# Input: timeStyle = 'UTC', 'LOCAL', the function will default to
#                     UTC Time if you pass in nothing.

def GetTime(timeStyle = "UTC"):

    if timeStyle == 'UTC':
        return ('UTC Time: ', time.asctime(time.gmtime(time.time())))
    else:
        return ('LOC Time: ', time.asctime(time.localtime(time.time())))

# End GetTime Function =============================


# Function: LogEvent()
#
# Logs the event message and specified type
# Input:
#         eventType: LOG_INFO, LOG_WARN, LOG_ERR, LOG_CRIT or LOG_DEBUG
#         eventMessage : string containing the message to be logged
```

```python
def LogEvent(eventType, eventMessage):
    if type(eventMessage) == str:
        try:

            timeStr = GetTime('UTC')
            # Combine current Time with the eventMessage
            # You can specify either 'UTC' or 'LOCAL'
            # Based on the GetTime parameter

            eventMessage = str(timeStr)+": "+eventMessage

            if eventType == LOG_INFO:
                logging.info(eventMessage)

            elif eventType == LOG_DEBUG:
                logging.debug(eventMessage)

            elif eventType == LOG_WARN:
                logging.warning(eventMessage)

            elif eventType == LOG_ERR:
                logging.error(eventMessage)

            elif eventType == LOG_CRIT:
                logging.critical(eventMessage)

            else:
                logging.info(eventMessage)
        except:
            logging.warn("Event messages must be strings")
    else:
        logging.warn('Received invalid event message')

# End LogEvent Function ===========================

        # Simple CSV Write Method
        # Without Library Assist

    D   def WriteCSV(fileName, MD5, match, category):
            if match:
                csvOut.write(fileName+","+MD5+","+ "*** YES ***"+","+category+"\n")
            else:
                csvOut.write(fileName+","+MD5+","+ "   "+","+""+"\n")
```

```python
# Main Script Starts Here
#
# Script Overview
#
# The purpose of this script it to provide an example
# script that demonstrate and leverage key capabilities
# of Python that provides direct value to the
# forensic investigator.

if __name__ == '__main__':
    # Mark the starting time of the main loop
    theStart = time.time()

    LogEvent(LOG_INFO, SCRIPT_NAME)
    LogEvent(LOG_INFO, SCRIPT_VERSION)
    LogEvent(LOG_INFO, "Script Started")

    # Print Basic Script Information
    # For MPE+ Scripts the length of the argument vector is
    # always 2 scriptName, path

    if len(argv) == 2:
        scriptName, path = argv
    else:
        LogEvent(LOG_INFO, argv + " Invalid Command line")
        quit()

    LogEvent(LOG_INFO, "Command Line Argument Vector")
    LogEvent(LOG_INFO, "Script Name: " + scriptName)
    LogEvent(LOG_INFO, "Script Path: " + path)

    # Verify the path exists and determine
    # the path type
    LogEvent(LOG_INFO, "Processing Command Line")

    if os.path.exists(path):
        LogEvent(LOG_INFO, "Path Exists")
        if os.path.isdir(path):
            LogEvent(LOG_INFO, "Path is a directory")
        else:
            LogEvent(LOG_ERR, path + " is not a directory")
            quit()
```

```
    else:
        LogEvent(LOG_ERR, path + " Does not exist")
        quit()


LogEvent(LOG_INFO, "Reading Hash Values to Search from: "+SRC_HASH)
LogEvent(LOG_INFO, "Creating Dictionary of Hashes")
```

E
```
    hashDict = {}
    try:
        with open(SRC_HASH) as srcHashes:
            # for each line in the file extract the hash and id
            # then store the result in a dictionary
            # key, value pair
            # in this case the hash is the key and id is the value

            LogEvent(LOG_INFO, "Hashes included in Search")
            LogEvent(LOG_INFO, "====== HASHES INCLUDED IN SEARCH =====")
```

F
```
            for eachLine in srcHashes:
                if eachLine != "END":
                    lineList = eachLine.split()
                    if len(lineList) >= 2:
                        hashKey = lineList[0].upper()
                        hashValue = ""
                        for eachElement in lineList[1:]:
                            hashValue = hashValue + " " + str(eachElement)

                        # Strip the newline from the hashValue
                        hashValue  = hashValue.strip()

                        # Add the key value pair to the dictionary
                        if hashKey not in hashDict:
                            hashDict[hashKey] = hashValue
                            LogEvent(LOG_INFO, hashKey+": "+hashValue)
                        else:
                            LogEvent(LOG_WARN,"Dup Hash Found: "+ hashKey)
                    else:
                        # Not a valid entry, continue to next line
                        continue
                else:
                    break
            LogEvent(LOG_INFO, "======    END HASH SEARCH LIST   ======")

    except:
        LogEvent(LOG_ERR, "Failed to load Hash List: "+SRC_HASH)
```

```
LogEvent(LOG_INFO, "=========== FILE SEARCH START ==========")

# Create Empty matchList and filesProcessed Count
matchList = []
filesProcessed  = 0

# Now process all files in the directory provided
# Including all subdirectories

for root, subdirs, files in os.walk(path):

    for curFile in files:
        # Create the full pathName
        fullPath = os.path.join(root, curFile)

        # Generate the hash for the current file
        # Default is to use MD5
        hasher = hashlib.md5()
        with open(fullPath, 'rb') as theTarget:

            filesProcessed += 1

            # Read the contents of the file and hash them
            fileContents = theTarget.read()
            hasher.update(fileContents)

            # get the resulting hashdigest
            hashDigest = hasher.hexdigest().upper()

        # Now check for a hash match against the
        # list we read in by checking the contents of the dictionary

        if hashDigest in hashDict:
            # If match log the match and add the match to the matchList
            matchDetails = hashDict[hashDigest]
            LogEvent(LOG_CRIT, "*** HASH MATCH File *** ")
            LogEvent(LOG_CRIT, "    MATCH File >> "+ curFile)
            LogEvent(LOG_CRIT, "    MD5 DIGEST >> "+ hashDigest)
            LogEvent(LOG_CRIT, "    CATEGORGY  >> "+ matchDetails)

            # add entry to match list
            matchList.append([curFile, hashDigest, matchDetails])

            # add entry to the csv file
            WriteCSV(curFile,hashDigest,True, matchDetails)
        else:
            # if no match simply log the file and associated hash value
            LogEvent(LOG_INFO, "File >> "+curFile+ " MD5 >> "+hashDigest)

            # add entry to csv file
            WriteCSV(curFile,hashDigest,False, "")
# All files are processed, close the CSV File
csvOut.close()
LogEvent(LOG_INFO, "=========== FILE SEARCH END ==========")
```

G

H

```
# Once we process all the files
# Log the contents of the match list
# at the end of the log file

# If any matches were found create a summary at
# the end of the log
if matchList:
    LogEvent(LOG_INFO, "")
    LogEvent(LOG_CRIT, "==== Matched Hash Summary Start ====")

    for eachItem in matchList:
        LogEvent(LOG_CRIT, "*** HASH MATCH File *** ")
        LogEvent(LOG_CRIT, "    MATCH File  >> "+ eachItem[0])
        LogEvent(LOG_CRIT, "    MD5 DIGEST  >> "+ eachItem[1])
        LogEvent(LOG_CRIT, "    CATEGORGY   >> "+ eachItem[2])

    LogEvent(LOG_CRIT, "==== Matched Hash Summary End ====")


# Record the End Time and calculate the elapsed time
theEnd = time.time()
elapsedTime = theEnd - theStart

# Log the number of Files Processed
# and the elapsed time

LogEvent(LOG_INFO, 'Files Processed: ' + str(filesProcessed))
LogEvent(LOG_INFO, 'Elapsed Time: '    + str(elapsedTime) + ' seconds')

# Now print the contents of the forensic log

with open(SCRIPT_LOG, 'r') as logData:
    for eachLine in logData:
        print(eachLine)
```

A Only one minor change to the template was required in Section A. The Python Standard Library module hashlib was added. This module will be utilized for all hashing operations. The library supports a wide range of hash algorithms, for this script we will use be using MD5.

B In the constants section of the template, we need to create a few new constants. Specifically:

SCRIPT_LOG: This defines the path where the log file will be created and written
CSV: This defines the path for the comma-separated value file

SRC_HASH: This defines the path to the file that contains the hashes to search. An example of the required contents of this file is shown here. The first column represents the MD5 hash string; the remaining represents a description of the what the hash is associated with. The last line should be END.

```
732A289B7DD8C7DD28D4D73ED2480BCF  Suspicious Image
40374D33463DFE213D31CCB0E1DEDC22  Proprietary Image
0CB2B38D5735F16EB7D87501BEC02001  Suspicous Camera
D41D8CD98F00B204E9800998ECF8427E  Malicious Code
18901D04BC17C3577EC9D37C103E317D  Suspicous File
END
```

C The code in Section C initializes (opens for writing) the comma-separated value file where the results of the hash operations will be written. During the initialization of the file, the header line is written which includes columns for: Filename, MD5 Hex Digest, Match, and Category.

D For this script, a new function, $WriteCSV()$, has been added to the function section. The new function will write a single row to the CSV file based on the parameters it receives. Since the output to the CSV file is a simple comma-separated text value, there was no need to import the Python Standard Library CSV module. The call of the function simply provides the path of the file being processed, the generated MD5 hex digest, True if the Match was detected, and the associated category string associated with the match. If a match is not found, the call provides False, and an empty string for the associated category.

E Moving on now to the main code and Section E. The hash values that make up the search must be read into a data structure within the script. There are many choices that could be chosen for this task. For our use, the best choice is to create a dictionary assuming that many hashes are likely to be needed and the quick identification of those hashes would be desirable. Dictionaries in Python are key/value pairs. In this case the key will be the hash value for the first column of the hash file (one per line), and the remaining text on that same line will be considered the value. The first step is to create an empty dictionary $hashDict=\{\}$ and then open the Hashes.txt using the $with$ operator in Python. This will allow us to process the entire file using the indented code under the $with$ clause. The $try:$ section is included in case an error is encountered when attempting to open the hashes.txt file. If any errors occur, the error will be logged and the program will terminate. Once the file is successfully opened, a $LogEvent$ is posted to the LogFile using the $LogEvent()$ function.

F Processing each of the lines of the Hashes.txt file comes next. As you can see the iterator method of Python allows us to process each line and write the code in an English language manner (i.e., $for\ eachLine\ in\ srcHashes:)$. Each time through the loop, the variable $eachLine$ takes on the contents of the next line in the hashes.txt file. The line is then split and processed to obtain a *hashKey* and *hashValue* string variables. The next step is to ensure that the key (the hexdigest) is not already stored in the dictionary, creating a duplicate entry. If it is not already in the dictionary, a new entry is created with the new key, value pair. This process continues until all lines in the hashes.txt file have been processed. It should be noted that each entry stored in the dictionary will also be written to the Log to record the scope of the hash search that was performed.

G Now that we have established the hashes to search for, opened the CSV and Log files, and obtained the path of the directory where searching is to begin, we are ready to perform the hashing of all the files contained in the target directory and any subdirectories that are included. We start by logging an event showing that the search has begun, and we create two new variables.

> *filesProcessed = 0*: Will keep a count of the number of files that were processed
> *matchList = []*: Will record any matches that are found in order to generate a summary

The next step is to walk the target directory and process each file. For this we use the *os.walk()* method that is part of the os Python Standard Library as shown:

```
for root, subdirs, files in os.walk(path):
```

This allows for the looping through each file within the target directory structure. From there the contents of each file is read, an MD5 hash object is created, and the hash of each file is generated. Since we create the hashDict that contains the hashes we wish to search for, a simple test can be performed to determine if we have a match:

```
if hashDigest in hashDict:
```

If so, the appropriate log events and CSV file entries are made. If not, the appropriate logging of just the Filename and Hash Values are written to the log and CSV, respectively.

Once all the files have been processed, the CSV file is closed and the log is written to indicate the search has completed.

H In order to highlight any matches beyond what has already been written to the log, a special summary section of the log is created if any matches were found. This will place the list matches directly at the end of the log for easy analysis. Finally, the number of files processed along with ending time and elapsed time are written to the log. At this point all that is left is to dump the log file to the console in order to display the results of the search.

Executing a Hash Search

In order to execute a Hash Search, we select the folder or complete filesystem of the associated MPE+ files. In Fig. 3.19, I chose the data folder of the Android filesystem and selected Run pythonScripter from the right click drop down. As before, this launches the pythonScripter and copies all the associated folders and directories to a temporary directory. The PF_HashSearch.py script is selected from within the pythonScripter as shown in Fig. 3.20.

FIG. 3.19 MPE+ select folder for hash searching.

FIG. 3.20 Select hash search Python script.

Once the script is selected and successfully loaded, the script is executed as shown in Fig. 3.21.

FIG. 3.21 Hashing search script loaded and select execution.

In order to provide a glimpse at the generated output, screen shots were taken of different sections of the output windows as depicted in Figs. 3.22–3.25. These depict the hash list summary, followed by a sampling of generated hashes and a match. Next, the summary page is depicted and finally the wrap-up showing the number of files processed and elapsed time.

In order to utilize this script, you need to create a hash search list. The format of this hash list is very simple text file. Here is an example:

```
732A289B7DD8C7DD28D4D73ED2480BCF  Suspicious Image
40374D33463DFE213D31CCB0E1DEDC22  Proprietary Image
0CB2B38D5735F16EB7D87501BEC02001  Suspicous Camera
D41D8CD98F00B204E9800998ECF8427E  Malicious Code
18901D04BC17C3577EC9D37C103E317D  Suspicous File
END
```

The other output of interest from the script is the CSV file. This can be found in the CSV defined directory—results.csv in this example, as shown in the Fig. 3.26. Opening the results.csv using Microsoft Excel as shown in Fig. 3.27 shows the output in tabular form.

The last step of the process is shown in Figs. 3.28 and 3.29. In the pythonScripter, the button Publish allows the results written to the console to be added to MPE+ environment. Once you Publish the results, you can go back to MPE+ and review the results under the Python menu option.

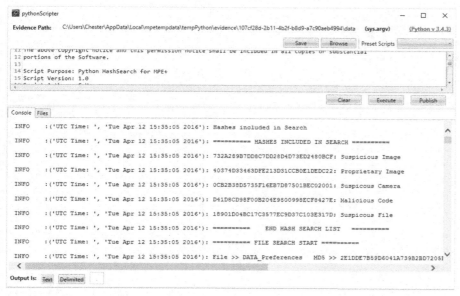

FIG. 3.22 Hash search Python script results part I.

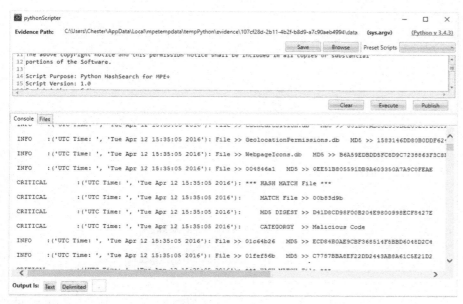

FIG. 3.23 Hash search Python script results part II.

FIG. 3.24 Hash search Python script results part III.

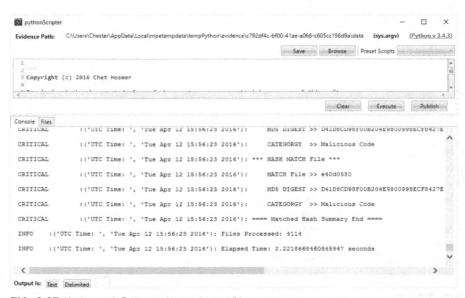

FIG. 3.25 Hash search Python script results part IV.

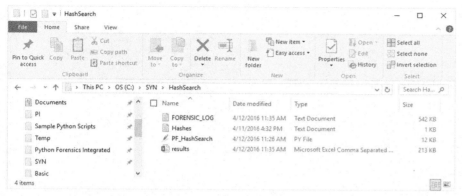

FIG. 3.26 Hash search Python script CSV file selection.

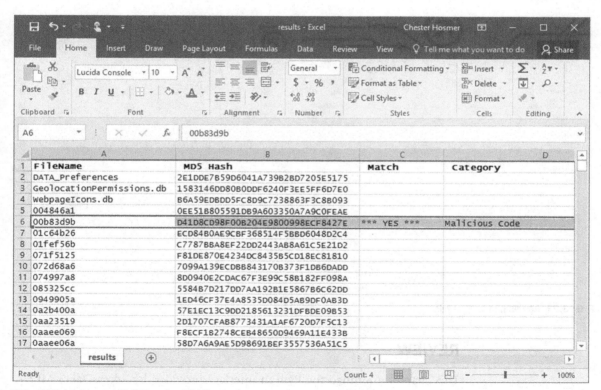

FIG. 3.27 Hash search Python script CSV file results.

FIG. 3.28 Select Publish button to post results to MPE+.

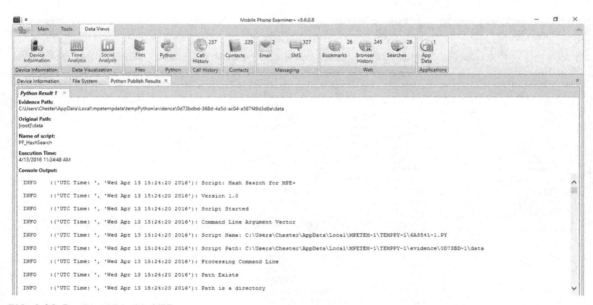

FIG. 3.29 Results published in MPE+.

REVIEW

This chapter examined the Python interface provided by AccessData's MPE+. The basic integration method was covered. Two script templates were demonstrated providing alternative methods of integration. Finally, the script

PF_HashSearch.py was developed, explained, and executed using an Android filesystem. The results of the search were examined and published back to MPE+ for future examination and analysis. The results were also written to a CSV file producing a more tabular result along with a detailed forensic log file.

CHALLENGE PROBLEMS

(1) Several enhancements and extensions are possible to the PF_HashSearch.py script.
   a. Allow the specification of additional hash methods (i.e., SHA-256, SHA-512) to be included as optional hash search methods.
   b. Expand the output to include meta data associated with each file encountered, that is, file size, MAC times, ownership, and file type.
(2) Using the same model presented for HashSearch, create new script to perform keyword searches.
(3) Develop a new script that extracts all photographic image files and orders them chronologically.

Additional Resources

[1] Python Standard Library, https://docs.python.org/2/library/index.html.
[2] AccessData MPE+ Users Manual, https://ad-pdf.s3.amazonaws.com/mpe/2015/02/MPE%2B_ UG.pdf.

## CHAPTER 4

Integrating Python With EnCase/EnScripts

INTRODUCTION

EnCase by Guidance Software is a leading forensic platform used by thousands of investigators and incident response practitioners. A key element of EnCase has always included the concept of investigators and developers expanding the scope and capabilities of EnCase. Traditionally, this has been done using two basic methods:

(1) Launching external file viewers
(2) Developing EnScripts (a proprietary scripting language) that provides developers with a powerful automation capability built into EnCase. EnScripts provide programmatic access to virtually anything that can be accessed manually through the standard EnCase interface, along with a rich programming environment to perform automation and analysis.

ENCASE INTEGRATION POINTS

Based on these two methods, I will be leveraging both of these to demonstrate the integration of simple Python scripts to enhance and expand on these core tools.

EnCase File Viewer Integration

EnCase File Viewer integration is traditionally used to leverage external tools that assist in viewing or interrogation specific file types such as: specific document types, images, multimedia files, accounting files, spreadsheets, and even encrypted content. To leverage this capability, you need to launch EnCase, open an existing case file (see Fig. 4.1), and then you would navigate to the desired file that you wish to inspect. Next, you would *right click* on the desired file, select *Open With*, and then select a desired viewer (see Fig. 4.2).

91

Integrating Python with Leading Computer Forensics Platforms. http://dx.doi.org/10.1016/B978-0-12-809949-0.00004-2

FIG. 4.1 EnCase v7 desktop screen.

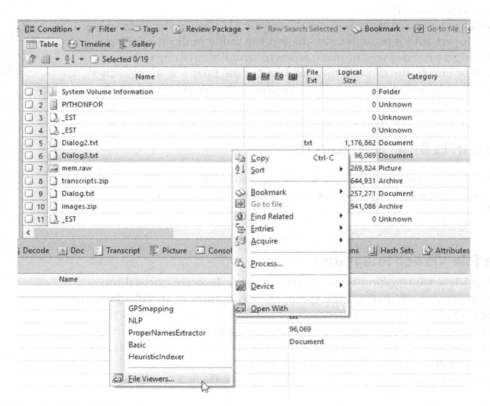

FIG. 4.2 EnCase v7 select desired file.

Before we jump right in and select one of the Python based viewers I have developed, we can examine the available File Viewers in order to review how to setup a new viewer or to edit and existing viewer to be used from within EnCase. You can do this by selecting the File Viewers option as shown in Fig. 4.3 and then select *File Viewers*. This will bring up a list of available File Viewers as shown in Fig. 4.3.

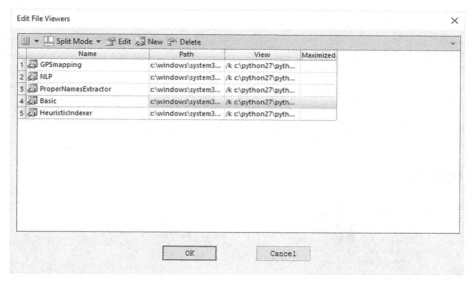

FIG. 4.3 Available file viewers list.

Next, by right-clicking on the Basic Viewer and selecting edit, we can examine the configuration of viewer, as shown in Fig. 4.4.

EnCase: Configuring a File Viewer
This will bring up the Edit Dialog Box as shown in Fig. 4.5. I have annotated seven aspects of the viewer that are important.

(1) The name assigned to the selected File Viewer by the user.
(2) The path to the application we wish to launch. Notice this is the Windows Command Line application rather than the Python application. We are going to launch Python from the Windows command line.
(3) The complete command that will be executed from the command line. Items 4–7 break down the command line options into the individual components.
(4) */k option*: This option instructs the Windows Command Process to execute the command then leave the command window open to allow

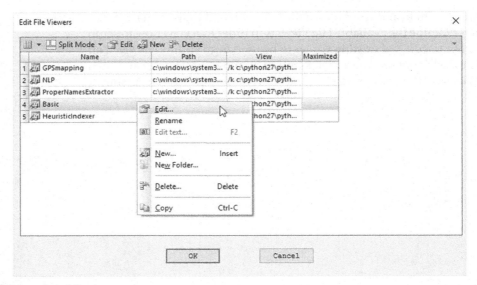

FIG. 4.4 Edit the selected file viewer.

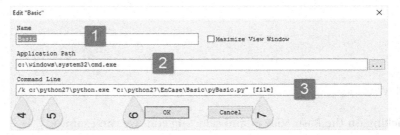

FIG. 4.5 Specifying the file viewer parameter.

us to review the results. Without the /k option, the command would just execute and then close the command window not giving us a chance to examine the results.

(5) This section of the command specifies the Python executable that is to be launched. In this example, we provide the full path to the python27 (i.e., Python v2.7 interpreter) executable.

(6) Next, we specify the full path to the specific Python script that we wish to execute. In this example, **pyBasic.py**.

(7) Finally, the *[file]* syntax inserts the full path to the file that is to be operated upon by the viewer; in this case, the Python script pyBasic.py.

EnCase: Launching a Python File Viewer

Now that the **Basic** Viewer parameters have been specified and are configured to launch Python and the associated **pyBasic.py** script we can launch the

viewer. In Fig. 4.6, we select the file **Dialog3.txt** and then right-click and select
the *Open With* item. We then select **Basic** specifying the specific viewer we wish
to launch. Fig. 4.7 depicts the output provided by the pyBasic.py script.

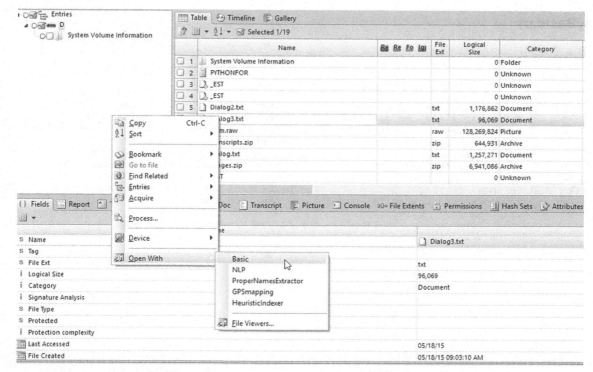

FIG. 4.6 Select and execute the **Basic** viewer.

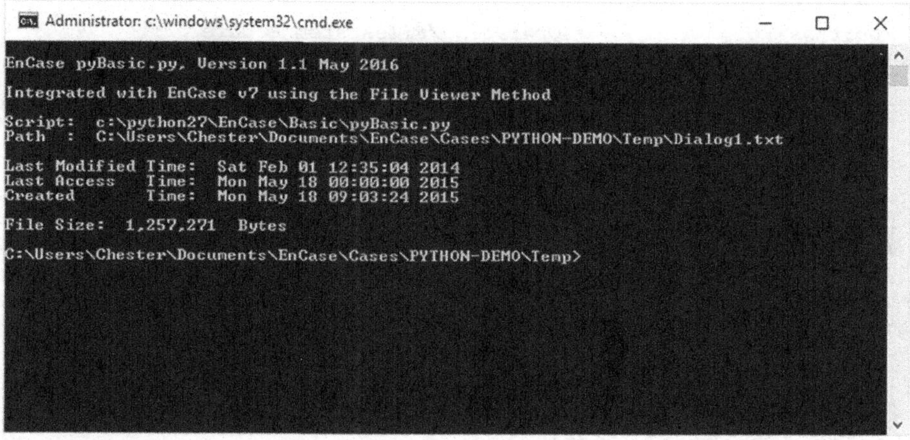

FIG. 4.7 Resulting python windows command line output.

pyBasic.py Script

The pyBasic.py script that was launched using the File Viewer method is outlined here:

pyBasic.py

A
```
'''
Copyright (c) 2016 Chet Hosmer

Permission is hereby granted, free of charge, to any person obtaining a copy
of this software and associated documentation files (the "Software"), to deal
in the Software without restriction, including without limitation the rights
to use, copy, modify, merge, publish, distribute, sublicense,
and/or sell copies of the Software, and to permit persons to whom the
Software is furnished to do so, subject to the following conditions:

The above copyright notice and this permission notice shall be included in
all copies or substantial portions of the Software.
Script Name:    pyBasic.py
Script Purpose: Python Template for EnCase Viewer+ Integration
Script Version: 1.0
Script Author:  C.Hosmer

Script Revision History:
Version 1.0 April 2016

'''
```

B
```
# Script Module Importing

# Python Standard Library Modules

import os                   # Operating/Filesystem Module
from sys import argv        # The systems argument vector, in Python this is
                            # a list of elements from the command line
import os                   # Python Standard Library : Operating System Methods
```

C
```
print
print "EnCase pyBasic.py, Version 1.1 May 2016"
print
print "Integrated with EnCase v7 using the File Viewer Method\n"

scriptName, filePath = argv

print "Script: ", scriptName
print "Path   : ", filePath
```

D
```
# get the file statistics
theFileStat =  os.stat(filePath)

# Print the File MAC Times
print
print "Last Modified Time: ", time.ctime(theFileStat.st_mtime)
print "Last Access   Time: ", time.ctime(theFileStat.st_atime)
print "Created       Time: ", time.ctime(theFileStat.st_ctime)
```

E
```
# Print the File Size

fileSize = theFileStat.st_size

print
print "File Size: ",
print "{:,}".format(fileSize), " Bytes"
```

A This section provides a place for you to include your copyright notice regarding the script. Since Python is intended to be an open source language, I have chosen this copyright notice for all the scripts that I develop. Your situation may differ, and the restrictions for use and distribution may also differ. However, you should clearly define this section if you intend for others to utilize and share your code.

B This section defines Python modules that will be imported into our script. This script only utilizes Python Standard Library modules. The script imports the os module, the time module, and from the sys module only imports argv.

os: The os module contains miscellaneous operating system interfaces. For example, use this if you wish to determine if a file or path exists, if you wish to navigate the file system or obtain the names of files. The module should contain all methods that are useful when examining the file system.

from sys import argv: In Python, you are able to import a whole module as with os above or in this case only import items from the module that are needed as done here. In this case, we only require the argument vector list (argv) from the system module.

time: The time module provides several key time-based conversion methods.

C This section prints out the header information which includes a brief description of the script along with the version and date. It also prints the full path of the script being executed, along with the full path name of the file being processed from EnCase.

$\boxed{\text{D}}$ This section utilizes the *os.stat()* method from the Python *os* module to obtain detailed information regarding the file name provided by EnCase. Then prints the modified, access, and created times of the selected files.

$\boxed{\text{E}}$ Finally, again using the results of the *os.stat()* method, this section retrieves the file size and prints out the size of the file in bytes. The formatted print statement inserts commas at the thousands separator points.

For experimentation purposes, you can run this script separate from EnCase by using the following example command line. This assumes that you have python 2.7.× installed.

python *pyBasic.py* **file.txt**

Where *file.txt* is a sample file.

This method of integration with EnCase has some basic advantages and some disadvantages. The advantage of course is simplicity of integration and experimentation. However, the major drawback is the decoupling of the script execution and results from EnCase. In other words, once EnCase launches the File Viewer (in this case, a Python script), execution is performed, and the results are only displayed in the Windows Command processor.

EnCase: Launching Python Using an EnScript

In many cases, a more direct coupling of EnCase and Python is desired. There are three significant benefits to a direct coupling approach.

(1) Multiple files can be selected and then processed by Python.
(2) The Python script results can be displayed directly in the EnCase Console Window.
(3) The Python script results can be written to and EnCase Bookmark allowing them to be permanently stored within the case.

The one disadvantage of this approach is that it requires the development and use of an EnCase EnScript. Development of EnScripts can be difficult for those without significant software development experience along with experience and training surrounding the EnScript language. However, to simplify this, I have adapted an EnScript originally published by James Habben of Guidance software. http://encase-forensic-blog.guidancesoftware.com/2014/09/encase-and-python-part-1.html. The advantage of using this adapted script is that you don't have to develop an EnScript from scratch.

The process of using an EnScript to launch a Python script and export multiple files for process is as follows: First, using the Evidence view of EnCase, you select the desired files for processing by the Python script as shown in Fig. 4.8.

	Name	Bs	Re	Fo	Ig	File Ext	Logical Size	Category	Signature Analysis	File Type	Protected	Protection complexity	
3	_EST						0	Unknown					05/1
4	_EST						0	Unknown					05/1
5	Dialog2.txt					txt	1,176,862	Document					05/1
6	Dialog3.txt					txt	96,069	Document					05/1
7	mem.raw					raw	128,269,824	Picture					05/1
8	transcripts.zip					zip	644,931	Archive					05/1
9	Dialog.txt					txt	1,257,271	Document					05/1
10	images.zip					zip	6,941,086	Archive					05/1
11	_EST						0	Unknown					05/1
12	_EST						0	Unknown					05/1
13	Volume Boot						565,248	Unknown					
14	Primary FAT						3,911,680	Unknown					
15	Secondary FAT						3,911,680	Unknown					

FIG. 4.8 Select files for export to python.

Once the desired files are selected, you choose EnScript from the EnCase menu bar. This will provide a list of available EnScripts. In this example, we choose the *SelectedFiles* EnScript from the dropdown list (see Fig. 4.9).

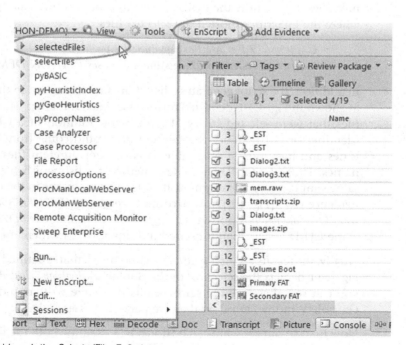

FIG. 4.9 Select and launch the *SelectedFiles* EnScript.

The results of the Python script launched by the *SelectedFiles* EnScript can be viewed by selecting in the *Console* Window of EnCase depicted in Fig. 4.10.

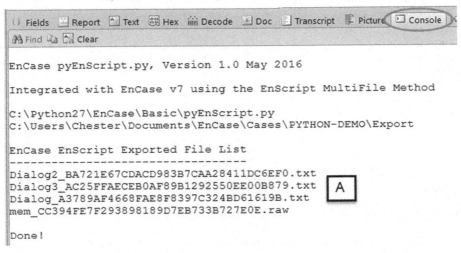

FIG. 4.10 Select and launch the *SelectedFiles* EnScript.

As you can see, the underlying Python script displays the informational messages that identify the Python script that was executed along with the path where the EnScript exported the selected files.

C:\Python27\EnCase\Basic\pyEnScript.py
C:\Users\Chester\Documents\EnCase\Cases\PYTHON-DEMO\Export

In addition, the script generates a list of the files contained in the Export folder as shown in Fig. 4.10 identified by the associated A marker. These are the same files that were selected in Fig. 4.8, with the addition of a Globally Unique Identifier or GUID. Since the selected files could come from multiple directories and locations, it is feasible to encounter different files with the same names. Thus, the GUIDs provide a method to distinguish files that have the same simple name. For example, the filename mem.raw in the original EnCase Evidence view (Fig. 4.8) now becomes *mem_CC394FE7F293898189D7EB733-B727E0E.raw when* exported. The *__CC394FE7F293898189D7EB733B727E0E* is the GUID assigned and inserted into the mem.raw filename.

Finally, the results are also written to a bookmark that is defined in the EnScript. Fig. 4.11 depicts the selection of the Bookmark *Python Selected File Results*. As you can see, these are the same results that were written and viewed in the Console Window, but now they are part of the Case File.

Now that we can see what can be done, let's examine both the EnScript and the Python script to dive into the details of how.

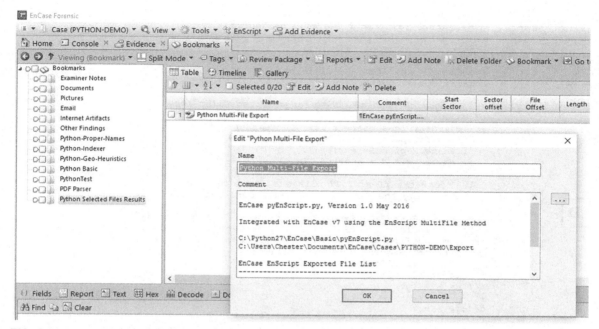

FIG. 4.11 Python export to Encase bookmark.

SelectedFiles *EnScript Details*

```
//
// selectedFiles EnScript
//
// Adapted from James Habben, Guidance Software Blog Post
//http://encase-forensic-blog.guidancesoftware.com/
2014/09/encase-and-python-part-1.html
//
//
```

```
A  // Main EnScript Class
   class MainClass {
     ItemIteratorClass::IterateModes IterMode;
     uint IterOptions;
     ItemCacheClass ItemCache;
     String ExportPath;
```

```
B  // Main Code Section

     void Main(CaseClass c) {
       if (c) {
           // Clear the console and
           SystemClass::ClearConsole(SystemClass::SHOWCONSOLE);
           Console.WriteLine("Starting Python SelectedFiles EnScript ... Please Wait\n");

           IterMode = ItemIteratorClass::CURRENTVIEW_SELECTED;
           IterOptions = ItemIteratorClass::NOPROXY|ItemIteratorClass::NORECURSE;
```

```
                    // Create the Export Path
                    // Where selected files will be copied

            ExportPath = c.ExportFolder();
            ItemIteratorClass iter(c, IterOptions, IterMode);
    C       ItemCache = new ItemCacheClass(c);
            LocalFileClass outputFile();

                    // Loop through all the user selected Files (check boxes)

            while (EntryClass entry = iter.GetNextEntry()) {
              String filepath, filename = entry.Name();
              filename.ReplaceExtension();
              filename += "_" + entry.GUID();

             // Create the final full pathname for each file
             // Including the GUID to mitigation duplicate filenames

    D          filepath.BuildPath(ExportPath, filename, entry.Extension());
               if ((FileClass inputFile = ItemCache.GetRawFile(entry)) &&
                   outputFile.Open(filepath, FileClass::WRITE)) {
                 outputFile.WriteBuffer(inputFile);
                 outputFile.Close();
                 inputFile.Close();
               }
            }
            delete iter;

            // Now prepare to launch Python and the specific Python Script

            String pythonPath = "C:\\Python27\\python.exe";
            String pyScriptPath = "C:\\Python27\\EnCase\\Basic\\pyEnScript.py";
            String pyArgs = ExportPath;

            ExecuteClass exe();
    E       exe.SetFolder(pythonPath.GetFilePath());
            exe.SetApplication(pythonPath);

                    // Execute Python and the specified Python script from the command line
                    // and pass the Export path value, where all the selected files
                    // have been copied

            exe.SetCommandLine(String::Format("\"{0}\" \"{1}\"", pyScriptPath, pyArgs));

                    // Write the results to the EnCase Console

            if (exe.Start(LocalMachine, 1000)) {
              Console.WriteLine(exe.Output());

                // Create a custom bookmark and store the results in the bookmark as well

              BookmarkClass bmf(c.BookmarkRoot(), "Python Selected Files Results", NodeClass::FOLDER);
    F         BookmarkClass note(bmf, "Python Multi-File Export");
              note.SetComment(exe.Output());
            }
                // Processing Complete
            Console.WriteLine("Done!\n{0}", SystemClass::LastError());
          }
        }
      }
```

A This section represents the main class for the EnScript. Also, key variables such as the iterator options and the Export Path are declared and will be used later in the EnScript.

B This section begins the main section of the EnScript, and the EnCase console windows is cleared. Also, the Initial EnScript message is displayed on the console to indicate that the EnScript has started and to announce the specifics function of the script. This is a good spot to modify the string to represent your specific script once you author your own EnScript/Python script combination.

C The main purpose of this section is to create the Export Path on the investigation machine. In this example, the export path created by EnCase is. *C:\Users\Chester\Documents\EnCase\Cases\PYTHON-DEMO\Export* This is based on the actual case that is being investigated. The base case folder was created during the Create New Case process with EnCase. The method simply creates the added *Export* folder.

It is important to note that the Export folder needs to be manually removed during each selection process as neither the EnScript nor the Python script deletes the contents of this folder upon startup or completion of the scripts.

D This section is one of the key aspects of the EnScript. The while loop traverses all the evidence in the case to find the items that are selected (i.e., checked) by the investigator. For each selected item, a slightly modified name is created (the GUID is inserted to ensure uniqueness), and the file is copied to the Export folder with the original file system metadata unchanged.

It should be noted for large cases the number of selected files that are to be copied to the Export folder could exceed the amount of available disk space.

E Once all the selected files are copied to the Export folder, the script prepares the command line that will be executed. In this example, the Python2.7 executable is chosen along with the script *pyEnScript.py*. If you wish to develop your own Python script, this is script line you would modify to specify the location of your Python script.

E Finally, the Windows Command line is executed with a short timeout (1000 ms or 1 second). In addition, the output is redirected to the EnCase

Console. Finally, a custom bookmark is created, and the output of the Python script is written to the bookmark.

As you probably have gathered, with this one EnScript you can pass files to process by any Python script you wish. All you need to do is make three simple changes to the EnScript for your use:

(1) Modify the Console Message to be appropriate for your Python script
(2) Modify the path to the Python script
(3) Modify the details (name and message) for the bookmark

Now that we have examined the structure of the EnScript, let's take a deep dive into the simplest Python script that produces the results depicted in Figs. 4.10 and 4.11. You can then use this simple Python script as a baseline for your own scripts.

pyEnscript.py *Details*
This Python script has only four moving parts that we will discuss.

```
# Guidance Test Python Application
# pyEnscript.py
#
# Author: C. Hosmer
# Python Forensics, Inc.
#
# May 2016
# Version 1.0
#


'''
Copyright (c) 2015 Chet Hosmer, Python Forensics


Permission is hereby granted, free of charge, to any person
obtaining a copy of this software and associated documentation
files (the "Software"), to deal in the Software without
restriction, including without limitation the rights to
use, copy, modify, merge, publish, distribute, sublicense,
and/or sell copies of the Software, and to permit persons to
whom the Software is furnished to do so, subject to the follow-
ing conditions:

The above copyright notice and this permission notice shall be
included in all copies or substantial portions of the
Software.
```

```
'''
```

A
```
from sys import argv      # The systems argument vector, in Python this is
                          # a list of elements from the command line
import os                 # Python Standard Library : Operating System Methods
```

B
```
print
print "EnCase pyEnScript.py, Version 1.0 May 2016"
print
print "Integrated with EnCase v7 using the EnScript MultiFile Method\n"
```

C
```
scriptName, filePath = argv

print scriptName
print filePath
print
```

D
```
fileList = os.listdir(filePath)

print "EnCase EnScript Exported File List"
print "--------------------------------"

for eachFile in fileList:
    print eachFile
```

A This section defines Python modules that will be imported into our script.

This script only utilizes Python Standard Library modules. The script imports the os module and from the sys module only imports argv.

os: The os module contains miscellaneous operating system interfaces. For example, use this if you wish to determine if a file or path exists, if you wish to navigate the filesystem or obtain the names of files. The module should contain all methods that are useful when examining the file system.

from sys import argv: In Python you are able to import the whole module as with os above or in this case only import items from the module that are needed as done here. In this case we only require the argument vector list (argv) from the system module.

B | In this section, the script prints out pertinent information regarding the Python script so that the results will be identifiable within the EnCase console window and ultimately in the associated bookmark.

C | This section captures and then prints the command line script information and passed argument (in this case, the path to the Export folder). Once again, this provides identifiable results for both the EnCase console and bookmark.

D | The final section demonstrates how to access and then print the filenames contained in the export folder. To do this, I utilize the *os.listdir()* method which generates a list containing the filenames included in Export Folder. I then simply demonstrate how to iterate through a Python list and print out each filename. This is a simple way to verify that the EnScript is copying the desired files to the Export folder and that the Python script can access them. This is likely a good thing to start with to identify the files that will be processed by the Python script. Now that we have the list we could easily perform whatever Python-based analysis that we can dream up on the files contained in the Export folder.

For experimentation purposes, you can run this script separate from EnCase by using the following example command line. This assumes that you have python 2.7.x installed.

python pyEnScript.py c:/

Where *c:/* is a valid folder name.

Note, there are a number of Python forensic scripts contained in my book Python forensics that could be adapted to interface with EnCase using either the File Viewer method or the EnScript method.

REVIEW

This chapter examined two distinct methods of integrating Python scripts with EnCase. The first used the File Viewer capability provided by EnCase to launch a Python script related to a single file. The second example employed both an EnCase EnScript along with a Python script to copy investigator selected files to an Export folder. Then using the Windows Command line, an argument was passed to the specified Python script identifying the folder where the selected files have been copied. The Python script then extracted the names of each file using a Python list.

CHALLENGE PROBLEMS

(1) Now that the door has been opened to interface Python with EnCase, what method do you find most useful for integrating Python with EnCase.

(2) Now develop a Python script of your choice to operate using the File Viewer method to analyze, display, carve, or examine the selected file.

(3) Now develop a Python script of your choice to operate using the EnScript method to analyze, display, carve, or examine a set of files selected within EnCase.

Additional Resources

[1] Python Standard Library, https://docs.python.org/2/library/index.html.

[2] Hosmer C. Python forensics: a workbench for inventing and sharing digital forensic technology, 2nd ed. Available from: http://www.amazon.com/Python-Forensics-workbench-inventing-technology/dp/0124186769/ref=sr_1_1?ie=UTF8&qid=1462319478&sr=8-1& keywords=python+forensics.

[3] James H. EnCase and python—part 1, http://encase-forensic-blog.guidancesoftware.com/2014/09/encase-and-python-part-1.html (accessed May, 2016).

## CHAPTER 5

Integrating Python With Leading Forensic Platforms

INTRODUCTION

We examined the integration of Python with MPE+ and EnCase in Chapters 3 and 4. In both of these cases, the integration was accomplished by launching Python scripts from within the forensic platform. In other words, the forensic platform was running and based on a case being investigated, and Python scripts were launched to perform additional analysis. We have classified these methods as *Direct Interface Integration*. In this chapter, we examine a different approach where the forensic tool has acquired evidence from a live running system and has provided results that require further analysis and investigation. We classify this as *Postprocessing Integration*.

For this example, I chose to examine US-LATT (USB-Live Acquisition and Triage Tool) developed by WetStone Technologies, Inc. (Fig. 5.1). The tool was initially funded by a research grant from the National Institute of Justice (NIJ) and then further developed into a commercial tool by WetStone.

FIG. 5.1 US-LATT secure USB device.

The goals of US-LATT were to deliver an easy to use tool that, with limited training, could be employed to acquire the most volatile data from running Microsoft Windows computers. US-LATT is focused on not only collecting evidence from a running system but also preserving and protecting the evidence once acquired. This is accomplished through the use of a secure USB device that automatically encrypts the acquired data and generates a one-way cryptographic hashes of all the data acquired. Fig. 5.2 depicts the login screen

109

Integrating Python with Leading Computer Forensics Platforms. http://dx.doi.org/10.1016/B978-0-12-809949-0.00005-4

generated by the secure USB device. Notice that an on-screen keyboard is presented in order to avoid using the system's keyboard anytime during the acquisition.

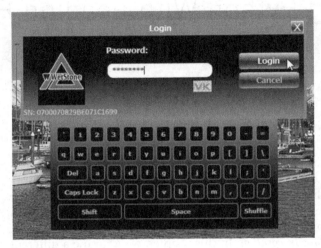

FIG. 5.2 US-LATT no keyboard required secure login.

Once the login is successful, the encrypted evidence and application volume is mounted (see Fig. 5.3).

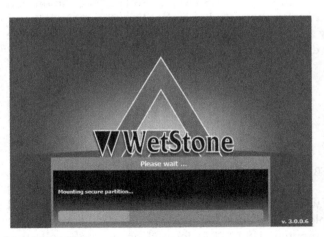

FIG. 5.3 US-LATT mounting the secure partition.

The US-LATT executable and case repository are stored in this secure partition. The US-LATT device is FIPS-140-2 certified, and 10 unsuccessful logins will zeroize the stored keying material. Thus if the device is lost or stolen, any evidence contained on the device will be safe.

Zeroization for many is a new topic, although the concept has been around for well over 2 decades in the context of cyber security and even longer within military systems. The basics are as follows: If tamper detection technology is employed (this could be physical tamper, door rattling, attempting an unusual number of logins, etc.), the device itself can selfdestruct or at least destroy the data contained in the device. Within typical FIPS-based encryption devices, this is done by simply zeroizing (writing all zeros) the encryption keys used to encrypt or decrypt the data. Thus the data itself held inside the device then become useless since the keying material necessary to decrypt the data has been destroyed.

US-LATT Configuration

Prior to utilizing using US-LATT to acquire evidence from a live running system, the device is configured and armed. The advantage of this is that no decisions need to be made during the acquisition process rather the policy that is configured drives the acquisition. This enables acquisition to be performed in the field with limited training. Fig. 5.4 shows just a portion of the configuration utility capabilities that allow the selection or deselection of system elements to collect.

FIG. 5.4 US-LATT configuration utility.

US-LATT Acquisition Walk-Through

Once the US-LATT device is configured and armed, the device can be deployed in the field to collect evidence. Various capacity devices are available; 32GB through 1 TB devices are available as of this writing, allowing for multiple acquisitions to take place using a single device. Evidence from each acquisition is stored separately on the encrypted device. US-LATT is then inserted into a target system, and the login process is repeated. The acquisition application is then executed by the users, and the dialog box shown in Fig. 5.5 is launched.

FIG. 5.5 Launching US-LATT acquisition.

The investigator then activates US-LATT with the *Run Triage* button. This starts the process of collecting the most volatile evidence first, as shown in Fig. 5.6.

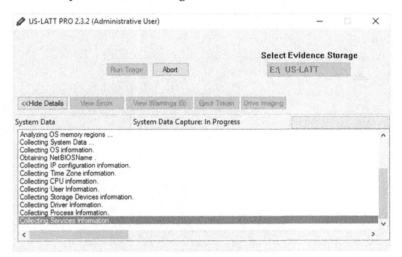

FIG. 5.6 US-LATT triage collection process.

US-LATT acquires discrete targeted evidence such as memory snapshots, running processes, running services, registry data, event logs, screenshots of all active applications (even if the windows are minimized), user information and activity, files, recent USB activity, application activity, and even logical disk images. The resulting data are stored with associated eXtensible Markup Language (XML) documents that detail the captured evidence. A detailed audit record is also generated that marks the chronological events that take place during the acquisition.

US-LATT Evidence Structure

Fig. 5.7 depicts the root directory of the mounted secure partition. The *CaseDirectory* contains data stored on the device from the various acquisitions performed by US-LATT.

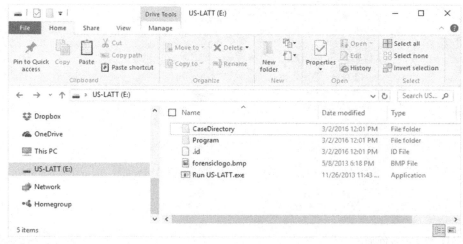

FIG. 5.7 US-LATT mounted secure partition.

Browsing into the CaseDirectory, we find folders labeled with the Computer Names that were acquired and concatenated with the time and date of the acquisition (see Fig. 5.8).

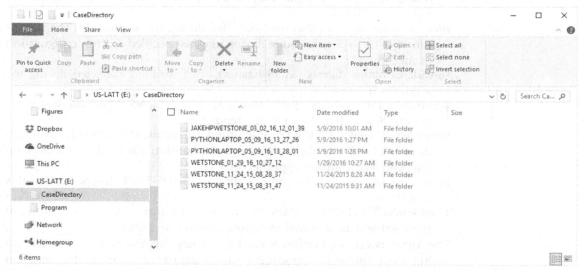

FIG. 5.8 US-LATT exploring the case directory.

Examining the contents of the acquisitions, we see a common folder structure as shown in Fig. 5.9.

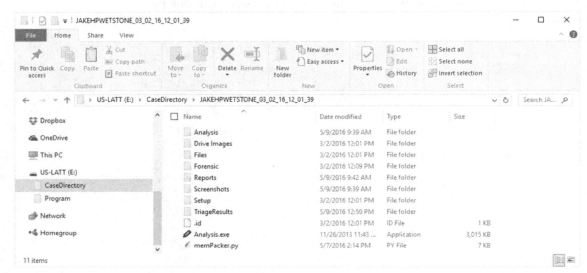

FIG. 5.9 US-LATT acquisition folder.

The contents of the acquired evidence and the associated information are stored in subfolders as follows:

Analysis Contains information such as timelines of user or web activity that are generated by the US-LATT analysis application.

Drive Images Contains raw (*dd* like) images of any drives that were imaged during the acquisition.

Files Contains any files that were collected during the acquisition. The specification of file types to acquire during triage is specified during configuration of the US-LATT.

Forensic Contains digests (MD5 hashes) of each object collected during the acquisition phase.

Reports Contains evidence pertaining to specific evidence. For example, photographs, Skype chat, web activity, reports, etc.

Screenshots If enabled during configuration, this folder will contain screen captures of all active applications (minimized or not), the taskbar, and desktop uncovered by running applications.

Setup Contains the specific configuration of the US-LATT that performed this acquisition.

TriageResults This folder contains the results of the triage operation including all the volatile data acquired including memory snapshots.

The **Analysis.exe** application is used to display the results of the acquisition within a web-browser environment. All the data acquired (with the exception of the raw data such as disk images and memory snapshots) are stored in XML format. This allows the contents of the data to be rendered within a browser using custom *stylesheets* associated with each data type, as shown in Fig. 5.10. As you can see, the amount and diversity of information collected during the US-LATT process is vast and comprehensive.

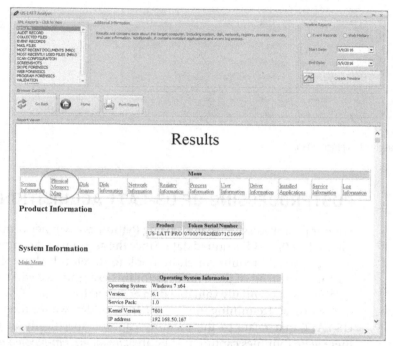

FIG. 5.10 US-LATT analysis application results display.

By selecting the link to the *Physical Memory Map*, Fig. 5.11 represents the specific memory map detected and subsequently captured during this US-LATT acquisition.

Finally, the **memPacker.py** Python script combines the memory snapshot sections into one continuous memory file. Since certain areas of physical memory cannot be read (due to kernel restrictions or because they point to memory mapped I/O areas that don't contain physical memory), the memory snapshots need to be stitched together filling these dark areas with zeroes. This allows for a complete memory map that would be compatible with other Python tools such as *Volatility* that perform malware analysis to process US-LATT memory acquisitions.

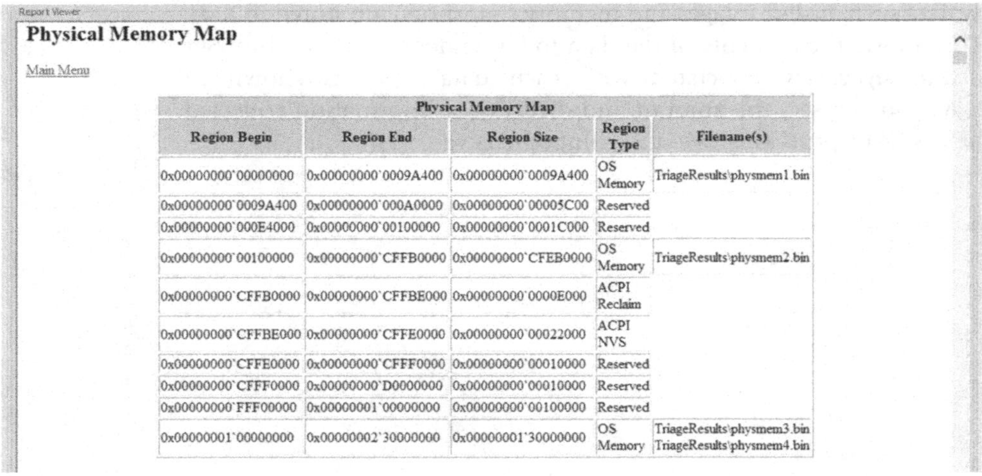

Report Viewer

Physical Memory Map

Main Menu

Physical Memory Map				
Region Begin	**Region End**	**Region Size**	**Region Type**	**Filename(s)**
0x00000000`00000000	0x00000000`0009A400	0x00000000`0009A400	OS Memory	TriageResults\physmem1.bin
0x00000000`0009A400	0x00000000`000A0000	0x00000000`00005C00	Reserved	
0x00000000`000E4000	0x00000000`00100000	0x00000000`0001C000	Reserved	
0x00000000`00100000	0x00000000`CFFB0000	0x00000000`CFEB0000	OS Memory	TriageResults\physmem2.bin
0x00000000`CFFB0000	0x00000000`CFFBE000	0x00000000`0000E000	ACPI Reclaim	
0x00000000`CFFBE000	0x00000000`CFFE0000	0x00000000`00022000	ACPI NVS	
0x00000000`CFFE0000	0x00000000`CFFF0000	0x00000000`00010000	Reserved	
0x00000000`CFFF0000	0x00000000`D0000000	0x00000000`00010000	Reserved	
0x00000000`FFF00000	0x00000001`00000000	0x00000000`00100000	Reserved	
0x00000001`00000000	0x00000002`30000000	0x00000001`30000000	OS Memory	TriageResults\physmem3.bin TriageResults\physmem4.bin

FIG. 5.11 US-LATT acquired memory map.

POSTPROCESSING OF US-LATT ACQUISITION

For our postprocessing analysis using Python, we will perform additional analysis of the US-LATT acquired data. Since the amount and complexity of the data is vast, it would require an entire book to develop Python scripts to perform postprocess on all of the data; thus for this example, we will focus on the most volatile and potentially valuable data acquired by US-LATT, which is the memory snapshot. Examining the *Triage Results* folder, we see the files generated by US-LATT that relate to the memory capture; specifically in this acquisition, there were four files captured. They are: *physmem1.bin-physmem4.bin* which correlate directly to the memory map shown previously in Fig. 5.11. I then executed the *memPacker.py* script to build a single complete image of the memory creating *memAll.bin*, highlighted in Fig. 5.12. This will be our target file for postprocessing during this chapter.

memScanner.py

The first postprocessing application we are going to apply is **memScanner.py**. This Python script is designed to perform searches of *memAll.bin* that produce lists of possible:

1. Credit Card Numbers
2. Email Addresses
3. Universal Resource Locators (URLs)
4. Strong Passwords

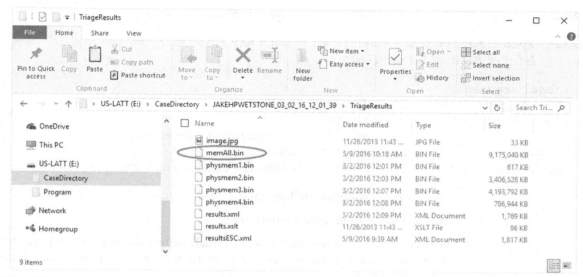

FIG. 5.12 Triage results folder highlighting *memAll.bin* file.

5. Social Security Numbers
6. U.S. Phone Numbers
7. Zip Codes with the associated City

A comma separated value file will be created for each category. To do this, I will be using compiled regular expressions processed by Python. This may sound like a straight-forward idea, however whenever dealing with regular expressions nothing is straight-forward. Building regular expressions that actually deliver quality results is the first challenge as most examples found on the Internet fall short. Next, integrating this into Python and processing a very large (8GB+ or larger), purely binary file adds additional challenges. The good news is that once this script is completed, the resulting Python script can be applied to even larger data objects produced by US-LATT or other applications, including larger memory snapshots, logical disk images, physical disk images, mobile phone images, etc.

For this script I'm using two source files. The first *memScanner.py* containing the main script, and the second file *pfDiscover.py* that performs the file handling, regular expression scanning, and produces the resulting comma separated value files. These two files should be placed in the same directory. Supporting the zip code lookup is a comma separated value file *zipdb.csv*, which also needs to be in the same directory as the *memScanner.py* and *pfDiscover.py*. The execution of the script requires the specification of certain command line arguments. You can obtain the information by typing the following command.

```
Chesters-MacBook:CH-05 TESTING Chet$ python memScanner.py -h
```

```
usage: Python Memory Image Scanner v .95 Beta May 2016
       [-h] -f FILEPATH [-c] [-q]
```

```
optional arguments:
  -h, --help       show this help message and exit
  -f FILEPATH, --filePath FILEPATH
                           path and filename of object to be examined
  -c, --csv              create csv file results
  -q, --quiet            run silent - no standard output results
```

The –f option specifies the file that you wish to scan.

The –c and –q arguments are optional.

Here is an example script execution on a small sample file specifying the output to comma separated value files and allowing for the generation of standard output messages.

```
Chesters-MacBook:CH-05 TESTING Chet$ python memScanner.py -f SampleFile.bin -c
```

```
Memory Image Scanner v 0.95 Beta May 2016
```

```
File Processed:     SampleFile.bin
File Size:          174,181 bytes
MAC Times:          ['Fri Feb 12 18:29:26 2016', 'Tue May 10 13:03:30 2016', 'Tue
May 10 10:35:01 2016']
```

```
Scanning Memory Image
. Scan Completed
Elapsed Time: 0.161141872406 Seconds
```

In addition to the standard output results, the script generates CSV files for each of the categories as shown here:

```
Chesters-MacBook:CH-05 TESTING Chet$ ls *.csv
csvCC.csv    csvPW.csv   csvURL.csv   csvZIP.csv
csvEmail.csv          csvSSN.csv  csvUSPH.csv
```

memScanner.py

```
' ' '
Copyright (c) 2016 Python Forensics and Chet Hosmer

Permission is hereby granted, free of charge, to any person obtaining a copy of
this software and associated documentation files (the "Software"), to deal in
```

Revision History

v .95 Beta   Initial Release (May 2016)
v .90 Alpha Initial Release Command Line Version (November 2015)

Writter for:
Python 2.6.x or greater (not Python 3.x)

e.g. usage

```
python memScanner.py -f memAll.bin -c -q
                     |              |  |_ Optional Argument to supress
                     |              |       standard out messages
                     |              |
                     |              |_ Optional Argument to create csv files
                     |                   for each category
                     |
                     |_ Mandatory Argument Filename to Process
```

Overview:

Script digests virtually any file Text or Binary (based on available memory) and attempts
to extract key data (possibly evidence) from the file. Current Support Includes:

- e-mail
- urls
- Social Security Numbers
- strong passwords (strings contain 6-12 continuous characters)
                    (with at least 1 upper case, 1 lower case and 1 number)
- Credit Card Numbers (AMEX, MC, Visa, Discover)
- U.S. Phone Numbers
- U.S. Postal Codes

'''

```
import argparse        # Python Standard Library to Parse Command Line
import pfDiscover       # Python Foreniscs Discover Module
import time            # Python Standard Library Time Module
```

```
#
# ------ MAIN SCRIPT STARTS HERE -----------------
#

if __name__ == '__main__':

    # Setup Argument Parser

    parser = argparse.ArgumentParser('Python Memory Image Scanner v .95 Beta
    parser.add_argument('-f',  '--filePath', required=True, help='path and
filename of object to be examined')
    parser.add_argument('-c',  '--csv',                     help='create csv
file results', action='store_true')
    parser.add_argument('-q', '--quiet',                    help='run silent
- no standard output results', action='store_true')

    # Process the Arguments
    theArgs = parser.parse_args()

    # Get the filename to process
    path = theArgs.filePath

    # Process the Optional Arguments
    if theArgs.csv:
        CSV = True
    else:
        CSV = False

    if theArgs.quiet:
        QUIET = True
    else:
        QUIET = False

    if not QUIET:
        print "Memory Image Scanner v 0.95 Beta May 2016\n"
```

```
    #Call the FileExaminer class with the filename provide

    FEobj = pfDiscover.FileExaminer(path)

    # Verify File is available and ready
    if FEobj.lastError == "OK":

        if not QUIET:
            print "File Processed: ", FEobj.path
            print "File   Size:    ", "{:,}".format(FEobj.fileSize), "bytes"
            print "MAC  Times:     ", FEobj.macTimes

        # Scan the file

        startTime = time.time()

        result = FEobj.scanMem(QUIET)

        endTime = time.time()

        elapsedTime = endTime - startTime
```

A

B

```
print "Scan Completed"
print "Elapsed Time: ", elapsedTime, "Seconds"


            # If this produced results
            if result:

                # Print to the Screen if not in Quiet Mode
                if not QUIET:

                    FEobj.printEmails()
                    FEobj.printURLs()
                    FEobj.printSSNs()
                    FEobj.printPWs()
                    FEobj.printCCs()
                    FEobj.printUSPHs()
                    FEobj.printZIPs()

                # Generate CSV files -c Argument provided
                if CSV:

                    FEobj.csvEmails()
                    FEobj.csvURLs()
                    FEobj.csvSSNs()
                    FEobj.csvPWs()
                    FEobj.csvCCs()
                    FEobj.csvUSPHs()
                    FEobj.csvZIPs()
            else:
                print FEobj.lastError

            #Clean up the object used for processing
            del FEobj

        else:
            print "Last Error: ", FEobj.lastError
```

The main script, memScanner.py, is meant to be very straight-forward and easy to follow. The script is broken down into three major sections: (A) command line argument parsing and setup, (B) execution of the scan, and (C) reporting of the results.

A For this script I'm using the Python Standard Library Module *argparse* to gather, verify, and set the operational modes (QUIET and CSV). The main argument is the target file that we will be processing during the scan and the –q and –c options set whether the results will be written to standard output (i.e., the console) and whether CSV files should be created for each category result.

B Next, I will be using the imported module *pfDiscover* that will perform the heavy lifting for the scan. The first step is to instantiate an object from the *FileExaminer* Class.

FEobj = pfDiscover.FileExaminer(path)

This creates the object *FEobj*. During the instantiation process, the path of the target file is verified, and the file system metadata regarding the file is gathered. In addition, the file is opened for reading. Finally, the *zipdb.csv* file is opened and loaded into a Python dictionary in order to later translate any zip codes that are found into specific city locations. Once these initialization functions are completed, the object is ready for use.

C Finally, basic information about the file to be scanned is printed to the console (provided that –q (the quite mode) is NOT selected). Then *FEobj. scanMem()* method is invoked which will perform the scan of the raw file and extract the pertinent data. Once completed the results will be printed to the console and/or written to the CSV file (if the options are selected). Note that the result printing and CSV writes are performed by methods contained in the *FEobj* as the data collected are stored within the object itself.

Next, we can examine how all this happens by examining the code in the *pyDiscover* module.

pyDiscover.py

```
'''
```

Revision History

```
v .95 Beta Initial Release (May 2016)
v .90 Alpha Initial Release Command Line Version (November 2015)

Writter for:
Python 2.6.x or greater (not Python 3.x)

pfDiscover Support File

Includes the FileExaminer Class

'''


# Required Python Import Standard Library Modules
import os              # OS Module
import re              # Regular Expression Modules
import time            # Time Module
import traceback       # raceback exception Module

# Psuedo Constants

MAXBUFF = 1024 * 1024 * 16    # 16 Megabytes defines the size of
                              # of the memory chunks read

# Class: FileExaminer Class
#
# Desc: Handles all methods related to File Based Forensics
#  Methods constructor:   Initializes the Forensic File Object and Collects
#                         Basic Attributes
#                         File Size
#                         MAC Times
#                         Reads file into a buffer
#          hashFile:      Generates the selected one-way hash of the file
#          destructor:    Deletes the Forensic File Object

class FileExaminer:

     # Constructor
     def __init__(self, theFile):

          #Attributes of the Object
          self.lastError = "OK"
          self.mactimes  = ["","",""]
          self.fileSize  = 0
          self.fileOpen  = False
          self.fileType  = "unknown"
```

```
self.uid         = 0
self.gid         = 0
self.mountPoint = False
self.fileRead    = False
self.md5         = ""
self.sha1        = ""
self.path        = theFile
self.sha256      = ""
self.sha512      = ""
self.zipLookup   = False

self.emailDict = {}          # Create empty dictionaries
self.ssnDict   = {}
self.urlDict   = {}
self.pwDict    = {}
self.ccDict    = {}
self.usphDict  = {}
self.zipDict   = {}
self.zipDB     = {}

try:
    if os.path.exists(theFile):
        # get the file statistics
        theFileStat = os.stat(theFile)

        # get the MAC Times and store them in a list

        self.macTimes = []
        self.macTimes.append(time.ctime(theFileStat.st_mtime))
        self.macTimes.append(time.ctime(theFileStat.st_atime))
        self.macTimes.append(time.ctime(theFileStat.st_ctime))

        # get and store the File size

        self.fileSize = theFileStat.st_size

        # Get and store the ownership information

        self.uid = theFileStat.st_uid
        self.gid = theFileStat.st_gid

        if os.path.isfile(theFile):
            self.fileType = "File"
        # Is this a real file?
        elif os.path.islink(theFile):
```

A

```python
        self.fileType = "Link"
    # Is This filename actually a directory?
    elif os.path.isdir(theFile):
        self.fileType = "Directory"
    else:
        self.fileType = "Unknown"

    # Is the pathname a mount point?
    if os.path.ismount(theFile):
        self.mountPoint = True
    else:
        self.mountPoint = False
    # Is the file Accessible for Read?

    if os.access(theFile, os.R_OK) and self.fileType == "File":

        # Open the file to make sure we can access it
        self.fp = open(theFile, 'rb')

        self.fileOpen = True
    else:
        self.fileRead = False
    try:

        # Required zipdb comma separated value
        # file containing zipcode to city lookup
        with open("zipdb.csv", 'r') as zipData:
            for line in zipData:
                line=line.strip()
                lineList = line.split(',')
                if len(lineList) == 3:
                    key = lineList[0]
                    val = lineList[1:]
                    self.zipDB[key] = val
            self.zipLookup = True
    except:
        traceback.print_exc()
        self.zipLookup = False

else:
  self.lastError = "File does not exist"
```

B

```
        except:
            self.lastError = "File Exception Raised"

    # Function to Iterate through a large file
    # the file was opened during init


def readBUFF(self):

    # Read in a bytearray
    ba = bytearray(self.fp.read(MAXBUFF))

    # substitute spaces for all non-ascii characters
    # this improves the performance and accuracy of the
    # regular expression searches

    txt = re.sub('[^A-Za-z0-9 ~!@#$%^&*:;<>,.?/\-\(\)=+_]', ' ', ba)

    # Return the resulting text string that will be searched
    return txt
```

C

```python
#searches file for patterns matching
# e-mails
# SSN
# URL
# U.S. Phone Numbers
# U.S. Postal Codes
# Strong Passwords
# Credit Card Number

def scanMem(self, quiet):

    if not quiet:
        print "\nScanning Memory Image "

    # compile the regular expressions

    usphPattern     = re.compile(r'(1?(?: |\-|\.)?(?:\(\d{3}\)|\d{3})(?:
                      |\-|\.)?\d{3}(?: |\-|\.)?\d{4})')
    emailPattern    = re.compile(r'[A-Za-z0-9._%+-]+@[A-Za-z0-9.-]+\.[A-
                      Za-z]{2,4}')
    ssnPattern      = re.compile(r'\d{3}-\d{2}-\d{4}')
    urlPattern      = re.compile(r'\w+:\/\/[\w@][\w.:@]+\/?[\w\.?=%&=\-
                      @/$,]*')
    pwPattern       = re.compile(r'[A-Za-z0-9~!@#$%^&*;:]{6,12}')
    ccPattern       = re.compile(r'(3[47]\d{2}([ -
                      ]?)(?!(\d)\3{5}|123456|234567|345678)\d{6}\2(?!
                      (\d)\4{4})\d{5}|((4\d|5[1-5]|65)
                      \d{2}|6011)([ -]?)(?!(\d)\8{3}|1234|3456|5678)
                      \d{4}\7(?!(\d)\9{3})\d{4}\7\d{4})')
    zipPattern      = re.compile(r'(?!00[02-
                      5]|099|213|269|34[358]|353|419|
                      42[89]|51[789]
                      |529|53[36]|552|5[67]8|5[78]9|621|6[348]
                      2|6[46]3|659|69[4-9]|7[034]2|709|715|
                      771|81[789]|8[3469]9|8[4568]8|8[6-9]6|
                      8[68]7|9[02]9|987)\d{5}')


    cnt = 0
    gbProcessed = 0
```

E

```
# Iterate through the file one chunk at a time

for bArray in iter(self.readBUFF, ''):

    # Provides user feedback one dot = 16MB Chunk Processed
    if not quiet:
        if cnt < 64:
            cnt +=1
            print '.',
        else:
            # Print GB processed

            gbProcessed += 1
            print
            print "GB Processed: ", gbProcessed
            cnt = 0
```

F

```
    # Perform e-mail search
    try:
        # email
        partialResult = emailPattern.findall(bArray)
        for key in partialResult:
            key = str(key)
            # Keep track of the number of occurrences
            if key in self.emailDict:
                curValue = self.emailDict[key]
                curValue +=1
                self.emailDict[key] = curValue
            else:
                curValue = 1
                self.emailDict[key] = curValue

    except:
        traceback.print_exc()
        curValue = 1
        self.emailDict[key] = curValue
```

```python
# Search for Strong Passwords
try:
    # Password
    partialResult = pwPattern.findall(bArray)

    for key in partialResult:
        key = str(key)

        upper=0
        lower=0
        number=0
        special=0

        for eachChr in key:
            if eachChr in "abcdefghijklmnopqrstuvwxyz":
                lower = 1
            elif eachChr in 'ABCDEFGHIJKLMNOPQRSTUVWXYZ':
                upper = 1
            elif eachChr in '1234567890':
                number = 1
            elif eachChr in '~!@#$%^&*':
                special = 1

        if upper == 1 and lower == 1 and number == 1:
            # Keep track of the number of occurrences
            if key in self.pwDict:
                curValue = self.pwDict[key]
                curValue +=1
                self.pwDict[key] = curValue
            else:
                curValue = 1
                self.pwDict[key] = curValue
except:
            curValue = 1
            self.emailDict[key] = curValue

# Search for possible SS#
try:
    # ssn
    partialResult = ssnPattern.findall(bArray)
    for key in partialResult:
        key = str(key)
        # Keep track of the number of occurrences
        if key in self.ssnDict:
```

```
                            curValue = self.ssnDict[key]
                            curValue +=1
                            self.ssnDict[key] = curValue
                    else:
                            curValue = 1
                            self.ssnDict[key] = curValue
            except:
                curValue = 1
                self.ssnDict[key] = curValue

            # Search for URL's
            try:
                # url
                partialResult = urlPattern.findall(bArray)
                for key in partialResult:
                    key = str(key)
                    if key in self.urlDict:
                        curValue = self.urlDict[key]
                        curValue +=1
                        self.urlDict[key] = curValue
                    else:
                        curValue = 1
                        self.urlDict[key] = curValue
            except:
                curValue = 1
                self.urlDict[key] = curValue

            # Search for Credit Cards
            try:
                # Credit Card
                partialResult = ccPattern.findall(bArray)
                # Keep track of the number of occurrences
                for key in partialResult:
                    key=str(key[0])
                    key = key.translate(None, '- ')
                    if key in self.ccDict:
                        curValue = self.ccDict[key]
                        curValue +=1
                        self.ccDict[key] = curValue
                    else:
                        curValue = 1
                        self.ccDict[key] = curValue
            except:
                curValue = 1
                self.ccDict[key] = curValue
```

```python
        # Search for Phone Numbers
        try:
            # Phone Number
            partialResult = usphPattern.findall(bArray)

            for key in partialResult:
                key = str(key)
                key = key.strip()
                if key[0] in '23456789\(':
                    # Keep track of the number of occurrences
                    if key in self.usphDict:
                        curValue = self.usphDict[key]
                        curValue +=1
                        self.usphDict[key] = curValue
                    else:
                        curValue = 1
                        self.usphDict[key] = curValue
        except:
            curValue = 1
            self.usphDict[key] = curValue

        # Search for valid US Postal Codes
        try:
            # Valid US Postal Codes
            partialResult = zipPattern.findall(bArray)
            for key in partialResult:
                key = str(key)
                # Keep track of the number of occurrences
                if key in self.zipDict:
                    curValue = self.zipDict[key]
                    curValue +=1
                    self.zipDict[key] = curValue
                else:
                    curValue = 1
                    self.zipDict[key] = curValue
        except:
            curValue = 1
            self.zipDict[key] = curValue
    return True
```

G →

```python
def printEmails(self):

        print "\nPossible E-Mails"
        print "================\n"

        sortedList = [(k,v) for v,k in sorted([(v,k) for k,v in
self.emailDict.items()], reverse = True)]
        for entry in sortedList:
            print '%5d' % entry[1], '%s' % entry[0]


  def printURLs(self):
      print "\nPossible URLs"
      print "=============\n"
      sortedList = [(k,v) for v,k in sorted([(v,k) for k,v in
self.urlDict.items()], reverse = True)]
      for entry in sortedList:
          print '%5d' % entry[1], '%s' % entry[0]

  def printSSNs(self):
      print "\nPossible SSNs"
      print "=============\n"
      sortedList = [(k,v) for v,k in sorted([(v,k) for k,v in self.
ssnDict.items()], reverse = True)]
      for entry in sortedList:
          print '%5d' % entry[1], '%s' % entry[0]

  def printPWs(self):
      print "\nPossible PWs"
      print "=============\n"
      sortedList = [(k,v) for v,k in sorted([(v,k) for k,v in self.
pwDict.items()], reverse = True)]
      for entry in sortedList:
          print '%5d' % entry[1], '%s' % entry[0]

  def printCCs(self):
      print "\nPossible Credit Card #s"
      print "=======================\n"
      sortedList = [(k,v) for v,k in sorted([(v,k) for k,v in self.
ccDict.items()], reverse = True)]
      for entry in sortedList:
          print '%5d' % entry[1], '%s' % entry[0]

  def printUSPHs(self):
```

```
    print "\nPossible U.S. Phone #s"
    print "=====================\n"
    sortedList = [(k,v) for v,k in sorted([(v,k) for k,v in self.usphDict.items
()], reverse = True)]
    for entry in sortedList:
        print '%5d' % entry[1], '%s' % entry[0]


 def printZIPs(self):

    print "\nPossible Valid U.S. Postal Codes"
    print "================================\n"
    sortedList = [(k,v) for v,k in sorted([(v,k) for k,v in self.zipDict.items
()], reverse = True)]
    # If the zipLookup Dictionary is available
    # Obtain the associated City
    # if lookup fails, skip possible ZipCode

  if self.zipLookup:
    for entry in sortedList:
     if entry[0] in self.zipDB:
        valList = self.zipDB[entry[0]]
        print '%5d' % entry[1], '%s' % entry[0], '%s' % valList[0], '%s' % val-
List[1]
    else:
     for entry in sortedList:
      print '%5d' % entry[1], '%s' % entry[0]



    def csvEmails(self):

            # Open CSV File and Write Header Row
            try:
                csvFile = open("csvEmail.csv", 'w')
                tempList = ['Count', 'Possible E-mails']
                outStr = ",".join(tempList)
                csvFile.write(outStr)
                csvFile.write("\n")
            except:
                print "Cannot Open File for Write: csvEmail.csv"

            sortedList = [(k,v) for v,k in sorted([(v,k) for k,v in
        self.emailDict.items()], reverse = True)]

            for entry in sortedList:
                outStr = ",".join([str(entry[1]), entry[0]])
                csvFile.write(outStr)
                csvFile.write("\n")

            csvFile.close()
```

H

```python
def csvURLs(self):
    # Open CSV File and Write Header Row
    try:
        csvFile = open("csvURL.csv", 'w')
        tempList = ['Count', 'Possible URLs']
        outStr = ",".join(tempList)
        csvFile.write(outStr)
        csvFile.write("\n")
    except:
        print "Cannot Open File for Write: csvURL.csv"

    sortedList = [(k,v) for v,k in sorted([(v,k) for k,v in self.urlDict.items
()], reverse = True)]
    for entry in sortedList:
        outStr = ",".join([str(entry[1]), entry[0]])
        csvFile.write(outStr)
        csvFile.write("\n")

    csvFile.close()

def csvSSNs(self):
    # Open CSV File and Write Header Row
    try:
        csvFile = open("csvSSN.csv", 'w')
        tempList = ['Count', 'Possible SSNs']
        outStr = ",".join(tempList)
        csvFile.write(outStr)
        csvFile.write("\n")
    except:
        print "Cannot Open File for Write: csvSSN.csv"

    sortedList = [(k,v) for v,k in sorted([(v,k) for k,v in self.ssnDict.items
()], reverse = True)]
    for entry in sortedList:
        outStr = ",".join([str(entry[1]), entry[0]])
        csvFile.write(outStr)
        csvFile.write("\n")

    csvFile.close()

def csvPWs(self):
    # Open CSV File and Write Header Row
    try:
        csvFile = open("csvPW.csv", 'w')
        tempList = ['Count', 'Possible Strong Passwords']
        outStr = ",".join(tempList)
```

```
        csvFile.write(outStr)
        csvFile.write("\n")
    except:
      print "Cannot Open File for Write: csvPW.csv"

    sortedList = [(k,v) for v,k in sorted([(v,k) for k,v in self.pwDict.items()],
reverse = True)]
    for entry in sortedList:
        outStr = ",".join([str(entry[1]), entry[0]])
        csvFile.write(outStr)
        csvFile.write("\n")

    csvFile.close()

 def csvCCs(self):
    # Open CSV File and Write Header Row
    try:
        csvFile = open("csvCC.csv", 'w')
        tempList = ['Count', 'Possible Credit Cards']
        outStr = ",".join(tempList)
        csvFile.write(outStr)
        csvFile.write("\n")
    except:
        print "Cannot Open File for Write: csvCC.csv"

    sortedList = [(k,v) for v,k in sorted([(v,k) for k,v in self.ccDict.items()],
reverse = True)]
    for entry in sortedList:
        outStr = ",".join([str(entry[1]), entry[0]])
        csvFile.write(outStr)
        csvFile.write("\n")

    csvFile.close()

 def csvUSPHs(self):
    # Open CSV File and Write Header Row
    try:
        csvFile = open("csvUSPH.csv", 'w')
        tempList = ['Count', 'Possible U.S. Phone Numbers']
        outStr = ",".join(tempList)
        csvFile.write(outStr)
        csvFile.write("\n")
    except:
      print "Cannot Open File for Write: csvUSPH.csv"

    sortedList = [(k,v) for v,k in sorted([(v,k) for k,v in self.usphDict.items
()], reverse = True)]
```

```python
        for entry in sortedList:
            outStr = ",".join([str(entry[1]), entry[0]])
            csvFile.write(outStr)
            csvFile.write("\n")

        csvFile.close()
    def csvZIPs(self):
        # Open CSV File and Write Header Row
        try:
            csvFile = open("csvZIP.csv", 'w')
            tempList = ['Count', 'Possible Valid U.S. Postal Codes']
            outStr = ",".join(tempList)
            csvFile.write(outStr)
            csvFile.write("\n")
        except:
            print "Cannot Open File for Write: csvZIP.csv"

        sortedList = [(k,v) for v,k in sorted([(v,k) for k,v in self.zipDict.items
()], reverse = True)]
        # If the zipLookup Dictionary is available
        # Obtain the associated City
        # if lookup fails, skip possible ZipCode

        if self.zipLookup:
            for entry in sortedList:
                if entry[0] in self.zipDB:
                    valList = self.zipDB[entry[0]]
                    outStr = ",".join([str(entry[1]), entry[0], valList[0],
valList[1]])
                    csvFile.write(outStr)
                    csvFile.write("\n")
        else:
            for entry in sortedList:
                outStr = ",".join([str(entry[1]), entry[0]])
                csvFile.write(outStr)
                csvFile.write("\n")

        csvFile.close()

    def __del__(self):
        return
# End Forensic File Class =====================================
```

The *pyDiscover* module is broken down into Sections A-H to highlight each of the key and unique methods and processing strategies employed. The code is well documented; thus I will keep the descriptions of each of the sections at a functional level.

A This section defines the empty dictionaries that hold the results found during the regular expression searches. These placeholders are initialized whenever the object is instantiated.

B The zipdb.csv file (if present in the source folder) will be read in line by line. The file contains current translations of zip code values into city locations. The result is a Python language dictionary that can be used to lookup possible zip codes extracted during the scan. Note that this list does change from time to time as postal codes are changed, new codes are created, or old codes are removed. There are many online resources available to download the latest postal codes.

C Python standard object types (int, long, strings, lists, etc.) are iterable. The language allows us to create methods or even new objects that are also iterable. This special piece of code uses the file to be scanned to provide an iterable method `readBUFF()`. The `readBUFF` method performs two import functions. (1) It chunks the file so to not exceed the available memory by reading in 16 MegaBytes (MB) at a time. (2) Regular expressions have difficulty in processing purely binary data outside of the normal ASCII character range, and these data can impact the accuracy of the regular expression search. Thus our trick to overcome this challenge and improve the efficacy of the scan is to replace or substitute these values in the buffer with spaces. This process returns a simple 16 MB bytearray as a result, thus eliminating values that are not useful during our search. As you will see in Section E, we use this method to process the entire file.

D This section defines the regular expressions we will be using for each of the scans that will be performed. Note that these are not simple off-the-shelf regular expressions rather they have been worked, reworked, and tuned to deliver better accuracy for our application. Note that I'm using the `re. compiler()` method to improve the performance of the expressions.

E As mentioned, Section E iterates the file under investigation one chunk at a time using the method we defined in Section C. Thus, with just one line of code, we can obtain the next chunk of data from the file and process that chunk. Again, this eliminates the issue with available memory when processing large files and improves the accuracy and performance of the regular expressions.

F Section F processes each of the regular expressions, (U.S. phone numbers, email addresses, social security numbers, URLs, strong password detection, credit cards, and zip codes) to generate probable values for each category. During the procession of each category, when a probable value is found the associated dictionary (defined in Section A) is updated. If the value already exists in the dictionary, the counter or number of occurrences is updated for that entry.

G This section exposes a set of methods for the object that will print the contents of the associated dictionary to *standard out*. Note: the dictionary will be sorted and the values with the highest occurrence will be printed first. There is one method for each category.

H This section exposes a set of methods for the object that will create CSV files for the associated dictionary. Note that the dictionary will be sorted and the values with the highest occurrence will be written to the CSV file first. There is one method for each category.

Full Execution of memScanner.py

The following is an abbreviated result of the execution of memScanner.py. To limit the time and output generated, I choose just a portion of the 9GB resulting file. The command line executed was:

*C:\Users\Chester\Desktop\CH-05 Testing>**python memScanner.py -f physmem4.bin -c***

Sample Output—reduced for brevity:
```
Memory Image Scanner v 0.95 Beta May 2016
File Processed: physmem4.bin
File Size:        805,830,656 bytes
MAC Times:        ['Thu Oct 22 10:43:39 2015', 'Wed May 11 10:17:19 2016', 'Wed May
11 10:17:19 2016']
Scanning Memory Image
. . . . . . . . . . . . . . . . . . . . . . . . . . . . . . . . . . . . . . .Scan
Completed
Elapsed Time: 905.318000078 Seconds

Possible E-Mails
================
   202 sean@wetstonetech.com
   180 time-nuts@febo.com
   160 cjeffcoat@allencorporation.com
   113 none@vmware.com
   110 measurementtime-nuts@febo.com
   109 geoff.barron@wetstonetech.com
   100 time-nutstime-nuts-bounces@febo.com

. . .Reduced for brevity

     1 support@poweradmin.com
     1 support@pcmicro.comM
     1 support@pcdynamics.comM
     1 support@netlimiter.com

Possible URLs
=============
   448 https://www.google.com/?gws_rd=ssl
   216 http://www.movietickets.com/purchase.asp?afid=goog&amp
   161 http://www.fandango.com/redirect.aspx?a=11584&amp
   149 chrome://browser/skin/menuPanel.png
   130 https://www.yahoo.com
   118 http://yahoo.com
   113 chrome://browser/skin/menuPanel-small.png
```

. . .Reduced for brevity

   1 chrome://browser/locale/browser.properties
   1 chrome://browser/locale/aboutPrivateBrowsing.properties
   1 chrome://browser/content/utilityOverlay.js
   1 chrome://browser/content/searchSuggestionUI.css
   1 chrome://browser/content/pocket/pktApi.js

Possible SSNs
=============
. . .Results redacted due to possible security issues

Possible Strong PWs
=============
. . .Results redacted due to possible security issues

Possible Credit Card #s
=======================
. . .Results redacted due to possible security issues

Possible U.S. Phone #s
=====================
 31 571-340-3465
 31 2015080623
 30 877-762-4043
 30 2015101405

. . .Reduced for brevity

  1 9611574360
  1 9611413706
  1 9611395007

Possible Valid U.S. Postal Codes
================================
1261 22222   ARLINGTON VA
1042 44444   NEWTON FALLS OH
 805 30223   GRIFFIN GA
 803 73947   KEYES OK
 797 29376   ROEBUCK SC
 732 29733   ROCK HILL SC

. . .Reduced for brevity

  1 00667 LAJAS PR
  1 00660 HORMIGUEROS PR
  1 00647 ENSENADA PR
  1 00636 ROSARIO PR
  1 00622 BOQUERON PR
  1 00601 ADJUNTAS PR

Resulting Directory—containing the generated CSV files:

```
05/11/2016  10:37 AM    <DIR>          .
05/11/2016  10:37 AM    <DIR>          ..
05/11/2016  10:37 AM             7,657 csvCC.csv
05/11/2016  10:37 AM           116,611 csvEmail.csv
05/11/2016  10:37 AM         3,444,327 csvPW.csv
05/11/2016  10:37 AM                96 csvSSN.csv
05/11/2016  10:37 AM           846,793 csvURL.csv
05/11/2016  10:37 AM           162,269 csvUSPH.csv
05/11/2016  10:37 AM           490,852 csvZIP.csv
05/10/2016  01:04 PM             4,647 memScanner.py
05/10/2016  12:33 PM            22,255 pfDiscover.py
05/11/2016  10:18 AM            14,612 pfDiscover.pyc
10/22/2015  10:43 AM       805,830,656 physmem4.bin
11/05/2015  12:17 PM           830,203 zipdb.csv
              12 File(s)    811,770,978 bytes
               2 Dir(s) 800,359,784,448 bytes free
```

Opening the csvZIP.csv file is depicted in Fig. 5.13.

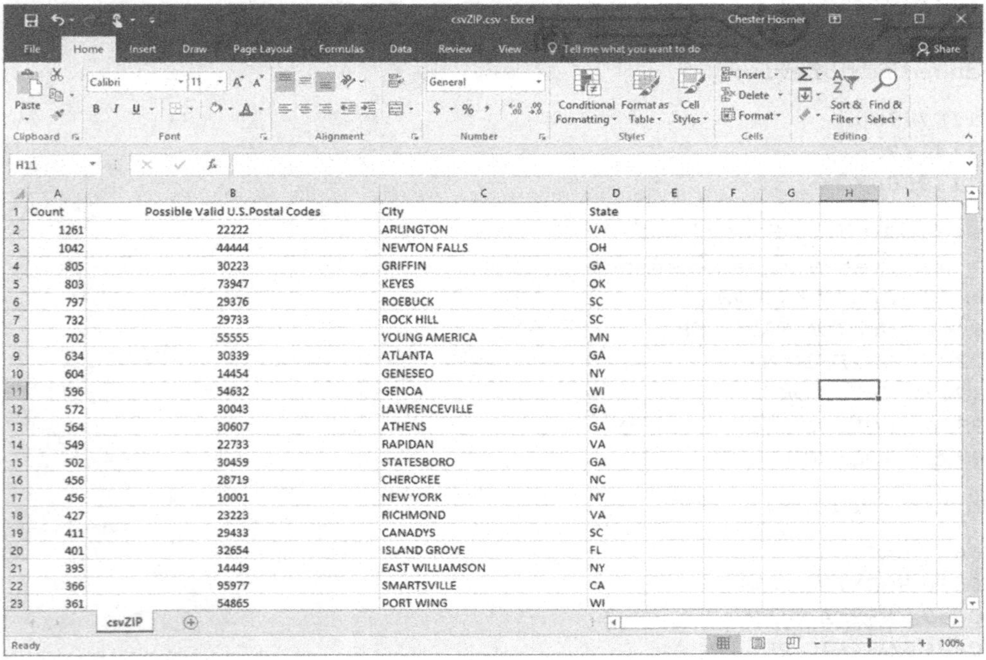

Count	Possible Valid U.S.Postal Codes	City	State
1261	22222	ARLINGTON	VA
1042	44444	NEWTON FALLS	OH
805	30223	GRIFFIN	GA
803	73947	KEYES	OK
797	29376	ROEBUCK	SC
732	29733	ROCK HILL	SC
702	55555	YOUNG AMERICA	MN
634	30339	ATLANTA	GA
604	14454	GENESEO	NY
596	54632	GENOA	WI
572	30043	LAWRENCEVILLE	GA
564	30607	ATHENS	GA
549	22733	RAPIDAN	VA
502	30459	STATESBORO	GA
456	28719	CHEROKEE	NC
456	10001	NEW YORK	NY
427	23223	RICHMOND	VA
411	29433	CANADYS	SC
401	32654	ISLAND GROVE	FL
395	14449	EAST WILLIAMSON	NY
366	95977	SMARTSVILLE	CA
361	54865	PORT WING	WI

FIG. 5.13 Sample csvZIP.csv file output.

REVIEW

This chapter demonstrated the postprocessing method of Python integration using WetStone's US-LATT product. We explored the use and application of US-LATT along with the structure of the resulting acquisition file. Based on this, I choose to develop the script memScanner.py that would postprocess the memory snapshot generated by US-LATT. The script uses a tuned set of regular expressions to uncover probable:

1. Credit Card Numbers
2. Email Addresses
3. Universal Resource Locators (URLs)
4. Strong Passwords
5. Social Security Numbers
6. U.S./North American Phone Numbers
7. Zip Codes with the associated City

The results are then printed to standard out and/or CSV files are created for each category.

The script is designed to run independently as well and can be applied to any file, memory snapshot, forensic logical or physical image, cell phone dump, or network trace to uncover the associated data.

CHALLENGE PROBLEMS

(1) Develop additional regular expressions and add them to the FileExaminer class. This will require the development of new regular expressions, adding of the new dictionary elements, functions to print the results and to write the results to associated CSV files.

(2) One significant enhancement to the script would be to leverage the multiprocessing library from the Python standard library to spread the processing of each regular expression search among the available cores. Since the current model processes each regular expression in sequence, this approach should significantly improve the performance characteristics of memScanner.py.

Additional Resources

[1] Python Standard Library. https://docs.python.org/2/library/index.html.

[2] US-LATT User's Guide Version 2.3. Available from: WetStone Technologies, Inc. upon request. www.wetstonetech.com.

## CHAPTER 6

Integrating Python With Leading Forensic Platforms

INTRODUCTION

Autopsy is a digital forensics platform and graphical interface to The Sleuth Kit along with other embedded tools and technologies that make up the software's underpinnings. The majority of the software has been developed and managed by Brian Carrier. It is used by law enforcement, military, and corporate examiners to investigate potential cybercrime activity. Autopsy is open source and runs on multiple platforms, providing plugin capability for Java and Python. For more information on the history, sponsors and partners responsible for Autopsy you can access the official website at: http://www.sleuthkit.org/autopsy/.

As mentioned, Autopsy provides a Graphical User Interface to the Sleuth Kit. Once you have successfully installed Autopsy on your platform and you first launch the application (As you can see I chose to install this on my Windows 10 Laptop, by following the directions provided on the autopsy website listed above.), you will see the image depicted in Fig. 6.1.

FIG. 6.1 Autopsy splash screen.

143

Integrating Python with Leading Computer Forensics Platforms. http://dx.doi.org/10.1016/B978-0-12-809949-0.00006-6

Next the user is presented with the options shown in Fig. 6.2. For this quick walk-through and integration example, I'm going to setup a brand new case.

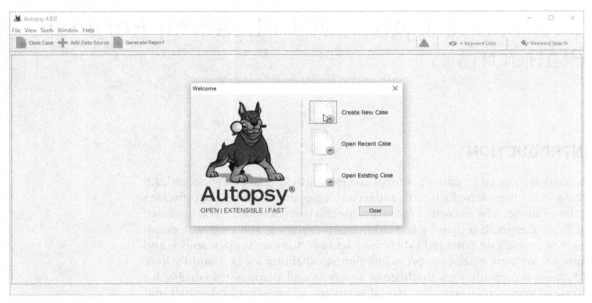

FIG. 6.2 Selecting Create New Case.

Next, I need to give the case a name and the base directory where it will operate. I'm going to use the default base directory supplied by Autopsy, and then I specify the case name, ProperNames. I chose this as that is the name of the script I'm going to develop (Fig. 6.3).

Next, I will specify the case number (since this isn't a real case, I'm specifying the PythonIntegration-Demo and the Investigator as me) (Fig. 6.4).

Since this is a brand new case, Autopsy allows me to add evidence to the case during the setup. I have preconfigured a small USB thumb drive with some test files and inserted into my laptop. I then select the local drive assigned to the USB as shown in Fig. 6.5. I labeled the drive "Autopsy" which is picked up by the software. I press Next to confirm this is the local drive I wish to use.

Fig. 6.6 then presents a selection of options called "Ingest Modules" that should be executed while the Data Source is loaded into Autopsy. (*Note*: we could have developed our Python script as an Inject Module and performed the analysis during the loading process.) I have chosen a different integration method; therefore, I will just select a couple of the basic Ingest Modules, namely, Hash Lookup and Recent Activity. This will ensure that hashes are generated for the files processed during the loading of the Data Source.

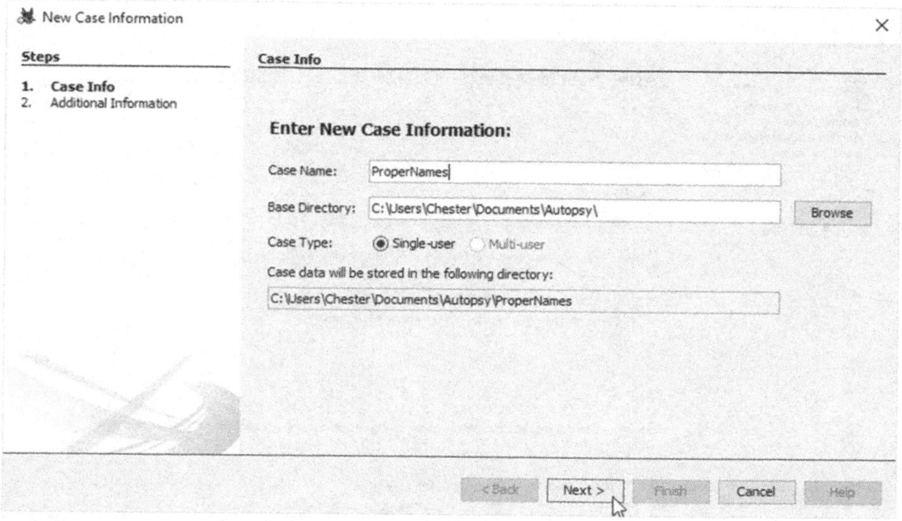

FIG. 6.3 Specify Case Name and Base Directory.

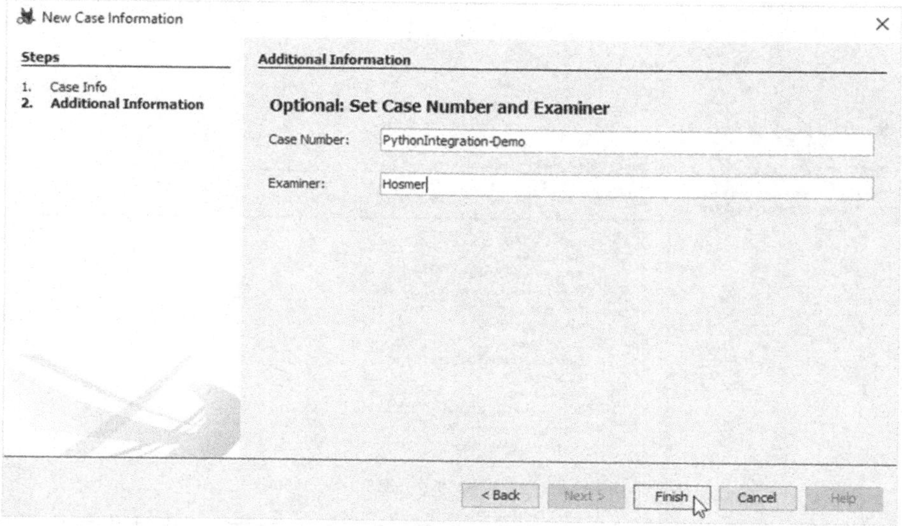

FIG. 6.4 Specify Case Number and Investigator.

Fig. 6.7 depicts the completed process and provides a tree control of the information collected from the small USB drive that I selected as my Data Source.

INTEGRATING PYTHON WITH AUTOPSY

Autopsy offers a couple methods for Python integration. The first is by creating an ingest Python module. There are a couple of different types of Ingest

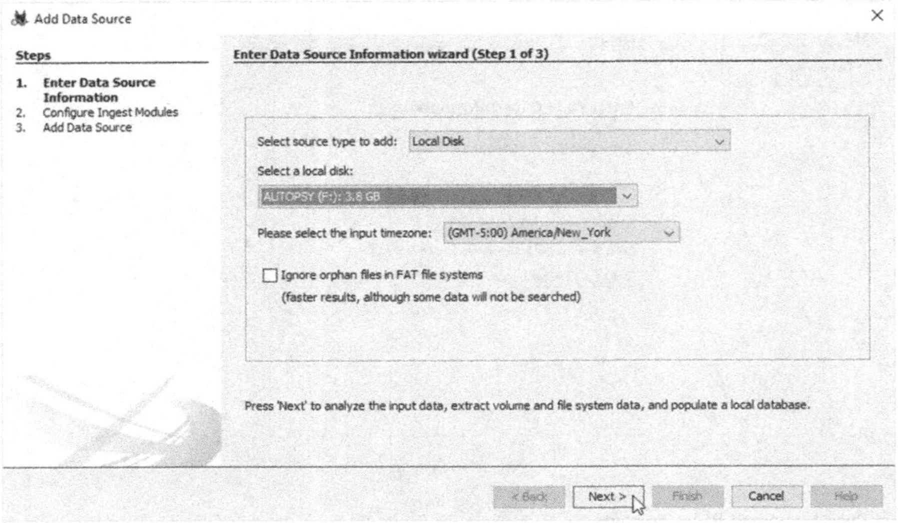

FIG. 6.5 Select Data Source to investigate.

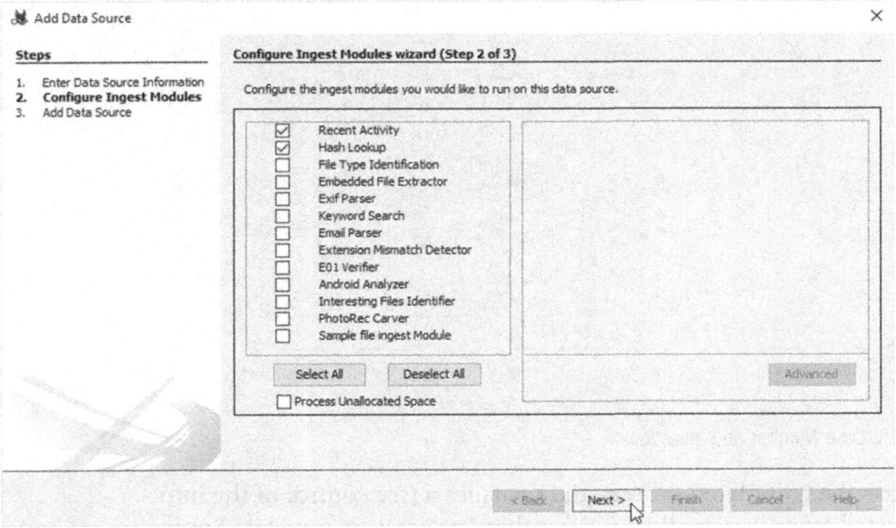

FIG. 6.6 Select Ingest Modules.

Modules that can be developed. The simplest is the File Ingest Modules which are automatically passed all files that are contained in the Data Source. As you witnessed in Fig. 6.6, users have the option to select specific Ingest Modules to execute when a local drive, drive image, files, or other evidence is added to the case.

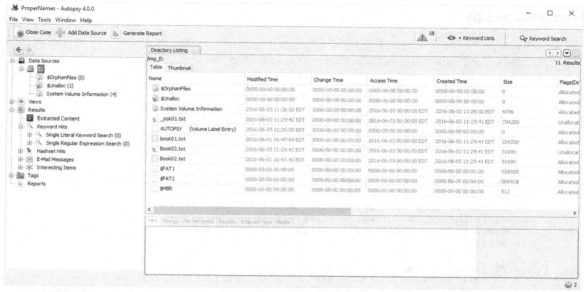

FIG. 6.7 Data Source Contents.

The Report Module

For this example, I'm going to tackle the second major type which is the Report Module. On the surface the Report Module may look a bit more complex, but because of the templates provided by Brian Carrier and the Autopsy team, most of the heavy lifting regarding the integration is done for you. To demonstrate this, my Report Module, which is called ProperNames, will leverage the provided Report Module template to integrate the module.

What Does ProperNames.py Do?

When examining ASCII text data during a forensic investigation, it is often useful to extract proper names and then rank those proper names by the highest number of occurrences. The Python language has built-in capabilities that will perform this extraction swiftly and easily. To demonstrate, I created a single Python script that will do just that.

But first, what is a proper name? Linguistics defines proper names as those words that represent a person, place, group, organization, or thing that typically begins with a capital letter. For example, proper names in a single word such as Robert, Jonathan, Kevin, Austin, Texas, Pentagon, Congress, or Microsoft can provide context and value to the investigation. In normal texts, these proper names are likely capitalized and quite easy to strip, identify, count, and sort. It should be noted that not everyone would routinely capitalize proper names; however, smart phones text messaging apps, e-mail programs, word processors, and even the Skype chat window automatically capitalizes these for us. Thus being able to extract and rank them can provide a quick look and provide perspective to an investigation.

properNames.py

A

```
'''
Copyright (c) 2016 Python Forensics and Chet Hosmer

Permission is hereby granted, free of charge, to any person obtaining a copy
of this software and associated documentation files (the "Software"), to deal
in the Software without restriction, including without limitation the rights
to use, copy, modify, merge, publish, distribute, sublicense, and/or sell
copies of the Software, and to permit persons to whom the Software is
furnished to do so, subject to the following conditions:

#
# This is free and unencumbered software released into the public domain.
#
# Anyone is free to copy, modify, publish, use, compile, sell, or
# distribute this software, either in source code form or as a compiled
# binary, for any purpose, commercial or non-commercial, and by any
# means.
#
# In jurisdictions that recognize copyright laws, the author or authors
# of this software dedicate any and all copyright interest in the
# software to the public domain. We make this dedication for the benefit
# of the public at large and to the detriment of our heirs and
# successors. We intend this dedication to be an overt act of
# relinquishment in perpetuity of all present and future rights to this
# software under copyright law.
#
# THE SOFTWARE IS PROVIDED "AS IS", WITHOUT WARRANTY OF ANY KIND,
# EXPRESS OR IMPLIED, INCLUDING BUT NOT LIMITED TO THE WARRANTIES OF
# MERCHANTABILITY, FITNESS FOR A PARTICULAR PURPOSE AND NONINFRINGEMENT.
# IN NO EVENT SHALL THE AUTHORS BE LIABLE FOR ANY CLAIM, DAMAGES OR
# OTHER LIABILITY, WHETHER IN AN ACTION OF CONTRACT, TORT OR OTHERWISE,
# ARISING FROM, OUT OF OR IN CONNECTION WITH THE SOFTWARE OR THE USE OR
# OTHER DEALINGS IN THE SOFTWARE.

# See http://sleuthkit.org/autopsy/docs/api-docs/3.1/index.html for
documentation

# Simple report module for Autopsy.
# Used as part of Python tutorials from Basis Technology - September 2015
```

B

```
import os
import logging
import jarray
from array import *
from java.lang import System
from java.util.logging import Level
from org.sleuthkit.datamodel import TskData
from org.sleuthkit.datamodel import AbstractFile
from org.sleuthkit.datamodel import ReadContentInputStream
from org.sleuthkit.autopsy.casemodule import Case
from org.sleuthkit.autopsy.coreutils import Logger
from org.sleuthkit.autopsy.report import GeneralReportModuleAdapter
from org.sleuthkit.autopsy.report.ReportProgressPanel import ReportStatus
from org.sleuthkit.autopsy.casemodule.services import FileManager
```

```
# List of English Language stop words.  These words may be
# capitalized in text documents, but provide little probative
# value, therefore they will be ignored if detected during the
# search. Stop words exist in virtually every language and
# many versions of stop words exist.  I have put this list together
# over time and found it to be effective in eliminating
# words that are not of interest.

stopWords =["able","about","above","accordance","according",
            "accordingly","across","actually","added","affected",
            "affecting","affects","after","afterwards","again",
            "against","almost","alone","along","already","also",
            "although","always","among","amongst","announce",
            "another","anybody","anyhow","anymore","anyone",
            "anything","anyway","anyways","anywhere","apparently",
            "approximately","arent","arise","around","aside",
            "asking","auth","available","away","awfully","back",
            "became","because","become","becomes","becoming",
            "been","before","beforehand","begin","beginning",
            "beginnings","begins","behind","being",
            "believe","below","beside","besides","between",
            "beyond","both","brief","briefly","came","cannot",
            "cause","causes","certain","certainly","come",
            "comes","contain","containing","contains","could",
            "couldnt","date","different","does","doing","done",
            "down","downwards","during","each","effect","eight",
            "eighty","either","else","elsewhere","end",
            "ending","enough","especially","even","ever",
            "every","everybody","everyone","everything",
            "everywhere","except","fifth","first","five",
            "followed","following","follows","former","formerly",
            "forth","found","four","from","further",
            "furthermore","gave","gets","getting",
            "give","given","gives","giving","goes",
            "gone","gotten","happens","hardly","has","have",
            "having","hence","here","hereafter","hereby",
            "herein","heres","hereupon","hers","herself",
            "himself","hither","home","howbeit","however",
            "hundred","immediate","immediately","importance",
            "important","indeed","index","information",
            "instead","into","invention","inward","itself",
            "just","keep","keeps","kept","know","known",
            "knows","largely","last","lately","later","latter",
            "latterly","least","less","lest","lets","like",
            "liked","likely","line","little","look","looking",
            "looks","made","mainly","make","makes","many",
            "maybe","mean","means","meantime","meanwhile",
            "merely","might","million","miss","more","moreover",
            "most","mostly","much","must","myself","name",
            "namely","near","nearly","necessarily","necessary",
            "need","needs","neither","never","nevertheless",
            "next","nine","ninety","nobody","none","nonetheless",
            "noone","normally","noted","nothing","nowhere",
            "obtain","obtained","obviously","often","okay",
            "omitted","once","ones","only","onto","other",
            "others","otherwise","ought","ours","ourselves",
```

```
"outside","over","overall","owing","page","pages",
"part","particular","particularly","past","perhaps",
"placed","please","plus","poorly","possible","possibly",
"potentially","predominantly","present","previously",
"primarily","probably","promptly","proud","provides",
"quickly","quite","rather","readily","really","recent",
"recently","refs","regarding","regardless",
"regards","related","relatively","research",
"respectively","resulted","resulting","results","right",
"run","said","same","saying","says","section","see",
"seeing","seem","seemed","seeming","seems","seen",
"self","selves","sent","seven","several","shall",
"shed","shes","should","show","showed","shown",
"showns","shows","significant","significantly",
"similar","similarly","since","slightly","some",
"somebody","somehow","someone","somethan",
"something","sometime","sometimes","somewhat",
"somewhere","soon","sorry","specifically","specified",
"specify","specifying","still","stop","strongly",
"substantially","successfully","such","sufficiently",
"suggest","sure","take","taken","taking","tell",
"tends","than","thank","thanks","thanx","that",
"thats","their","theirs","them","themselves","then",
"thence","there","thereafter","thereby","thered",
"therefore","therein","thereof","therere",
"theres","thereto","thereupon","there've","these",
"they","think","this","those","thou","though","thought",
"thousand","through","throughout","thru","thus",
"together","took","toward","towards","tried","tries",
"truly","trying","twice","under","unfortunately",
"unless","unlike","unlikely","until","unto","upon",
"used","useful","usefully","usefulness","uses","using",
"usually","value","various","very","want","wants",
"was","wasnt","welcome","went","were","what","whatever",
"when","whence","whenever","where", "whereafter",
"whereas",
"whereby","wherein","wheres","whereupon","wherever",
"whether","which","while","whim","whither","whod",
"whoever","whole","whom","whomever","whos","whose",
"widely","willing","wish","with","within","without",
"wont","words","world","would","wouldnt",
"your","youre","yours","yourself","yourselves"]
```

```
####################
# Function
# Name: ExtractProperNames
# Purpose: Extract possible proper names from the passed string
# Input: string
# Return: Dictionary of possible Proper Names along with the number of
#          of occurrences as a key, value pair
# Usage: theDictionary = ExtractProperNames('John is from Alaska')
####################

def ExtractProperNames(theBuffer):

    # Prepare the string (strip formatting and special characters)
    # You can extend the set of allowed characters by adding to the string
    # Note 1: this example assumes ASCII characters not unicode
    # Note 2: You can expand the allowed ASCII characters that you
    #         choose to include for valid proper name searches
    #         by modifying this string.  For this example I have kept
    #         the list simple.

    allowedCharacters ="ABCDEFGHIJKLMNOPQRSTUVWXYZabcdefghijklmnopqrstuvwxyz"

    finalString = ''

    # Notice that you can write Python like English if you choose your
    #     words carefully

    # Process each character in the theString passed to the function

    for eachCharacter in theBuffer:

        # Check to see if the character is in the allowedCharacter string
        if eachCharacter in allowedCharacters:
            # Yes, then add the character to the finalString
            finalString = finalString + eachCharacter
        else:
            # otherwise replace the not allowed character
            #     with a space
            finalString = finalString + ' '
```

```
    # Now that we only have allowed characters or spaces in finalString
    #     we can use the built in Python string.split() method
    # This one line will create a list of words contained in the finalString

    wordList = finalString.split()

    # Now, let's determine which words are possible proper names
    #     and create a list of them.

    # We start by declaring an empty list

    properNameList = []
```

D

E

```
          # For this example we will assume words are possible proper names
          # if they are in title case and they meet certain length requirements
          # We will use a Min Length of 4 and a Max Length of 20

          # To do this, we loop through each word in the word list
          #     and if the word is in title case and the word meets
          #     our minimum/maximum size limits we add the word to
          #     the properNameList
          # We utilize the Python built in string method string.istitle()
          #
          # Note: I'm setting minimum and maximum word lengths that
          #       will be considered proper names.  You can adjust these
          #       psuedo constants for your situation.  Note if you make
          #       the MIN_SIZE smaller you should also update the StopWord
          #       list to include smaller stop words.

          MIN_SIZE = 4
          MAX_SIZE = 20

          for eachWord in wordList:

              if eachWord.istitle() and len(eachWord) >= MIN_SIZE and
                              len(eachWord) <= MAX_SIZE:

                  # if the word meets the specified conditions we add it
                  # and it is not a common stop word
                  # we add it to the properNameList

                  if eachWord.lower() not in stopWords:
                      properNameList.append(eachWord)
              else:
                  # otherwise we loop to the next word
                  continue
```
```
      # Note this list will likely contain duplicates to deal with this
      #     and to determine the number of times a proper name is used
      #     we will create a Python Dictionary

      # The Dictionary will contain a key, value pair.
      # The key will be the proper name and value is the number of occurrences
      #     found in the text

      # Create an empty dictionary
      properNamesDictionary = {}

      # Next we loop through the properNamesList
      for eachName in properNameList:

          # if the name is already in the dictionary
          # the name has been processed increment the number
          # of occurrences, otherwise add a new entry setting
          # the occurrences to 1

          if eachName in properNamesDictionary:
              cnt = properNamesDictionary[eachName]
              properNamesDictionary[eachName] = cnt+1
          else:
              properNamesDictionary[eachName] = 1

      # Once all the words have been processed
      # the function returns the created properNames Dictionary

      return properNamesDictionary

# End Extract Proper Names Function
```

F

G

```
# Class responsible for defining module metadata and logic
class CSVReportModule(GeneralReportModuleAdapter):

    # This defines the Report name
    moduleName = "Proper Names Report"

    _logger = None
    def log(self, level, msg):
        if _logger == None:
            _logger = Logger.getLogger(self.moduleName)

        self._logger.logp(level, self.__class__.__name__,
inspect.stack()[1][3], msg)

    def getName(self):
        return self.moduleName

    def getDescription(self):
        return "Extracts Possible Proper Names"

    def getRelativeFilePath(self):
        return "prop.txt"
```

```
    def generateReport(self, baseReportDir, progressBar):

        # Open the output file.
        fileName = os.path.join(baseReportDir, self.getRelativeFilePath())
        report = open(fileName, 'w')

        # Query the database for the files (ignore the directories)
        sleuthkitCase = Case.getCurrentCase().getSleuthkitCase()
        files = sleuthkitCase.findAllFilesWhere("NOT meta_type = " +
str(TskData.TSK_FS_META_TYPE_ENUM.TSK_FS_META_TYPE_DIR.getValue()))

        # Setup progress Indicator
        progressBar.setIndeterminate(False)
        progressBar.start()
        progressBar.setMaximumProgress(len(files))
```

```
       for file in files:
              # For this script I will limit the processing
              # to files with .txt extensions only

              if file.getName().lower().endswith(".txt"):

                    # Setup to Read the contents of the file.

                    # Create a Python string to hold the file contents
                    # for processing

                    fileStringBuffer = ''

                    # Setup an inputStream to read the file
                    inputStream = ReadContentInputStream(file)

                    # Setup a jarry buffer to read chunks of the file
                    # we will read 1024 byte chunks

                    buffer = jarray.zeros(1024, "b")
```

J

```
# Attempt to read in the first Chunk
                    bytesRead = inputStream.read(buffer)

                    # Continue reading until finished reading
                    # the file indicated by -1 return from
                    # the inputStream.read() method

                    while (bytesRead != -1):

                         for eachItem in buffer:
                               # Now extract only potential ascii characters
                               # from the
                               # buffer and build the final Python string
                               # that we will process.

                               if eachItem >= 0 and eachItem <= 255:
                                    fileStringBuffer = fileStringBuffer +
                                                        chr(eachItem)

                         # Read the next file Chunk
                         bytesRead = inputStream.read(buffer)

                    # Once the complete file has been read and the
                    # possible ASCII characters have been extracted

                    # The ExtractProperNames Function
                    # will process the contents of the file
                    # the result will be returned as a Python
                    # dictionary object

                    properNamesDictionary = ExtractProperNames(fileStringBuffer)
```

K

```
        # For each file processed
        # Write the information to the Report
        # File Name, along with each possible proper name
        # found, with highest occurring words order

        report.write("\n\nProcessing File: "+ file.getUniquePath() +
                            "\n\n")
        report.write("Possible Name        Occurrences \n")
        report.write("------------------------------- \n")

        for eachName in sorted(properNamesDictionary,
                            key=properNamesDictionary.get,
                            reverse=True):

            theName = '{:20}'.format(eachName)
            theCnt  = '{:5d}'.format(properNamesDictionary[eachName])
            report.write(theName + theCnt + "\n")

    # Increment the progress bar for each
    # file processed
    progressBar.increment()


    # Process the Next File

    # Close the report and post ProgressBar Complete
    progressBar.complete(ReportStatus.COMPLETE)
    report.close()

    # Add the report to the Case
    Case.getCurrentCase().addReport(fileName, self.moduleName,
                            "Prop Report")
```

L

M

Since this script is tightly integrated with Autopsy, it is not possible to execute this script independently without modification.

A This script contains actually two copyright notices as the original template
was created by the Autopsy team. As you can see, it allows free use and distribution of the template. In addition, I have added my copyright notice, which
also provides open usage of the example provided here, again provided that the
copyright message is included in any subsequent use.

B The scope of imported modules used in this example comes from the direct
integration with Autopsy. Once Autopsy is installed, the imported modules are

directly available and do not require any action by the user. The only additional modules included are from the Python Standard Library, which are already available once Python is installed. It should be noted that Python 2.7.×× is recommended for compatibility.

C This section creates a list of the most popular English language stop words.

Stop words are commonly used in natural language processing as a filter. In this example, I'm using the stop word list to remove capitalized words that have little or in most cases no investigative value. It should be noted that I chose to include stop words with a length of four characters and up, as I define the minimum word length to be four. In some instances, you may wish to include three or even two letter words. If you modify the code to allow these for shorter words, then it would be advisable to add the appropriate two or three character stop words to the list.

D The *ExtractProperNames()* function represents the core processing algorithm for this script. In the first step, I create an allowed character list. You can also expand this list to allow additional characters to be considered. For example, you may wish to have all apostrophes or hyphens included in proper names. For this example, I only included the A-Z and a-z. Next, I create an empty string that will hold the final set of allowed characters. I then process each character and replace not allowed chara -cters with spaces. This will setup the string for easy processing with the split method.

E Once the final string is prepared, I utilize the string function split to create a Python list named *wordList*.

wordList = finalString.split()

This function will use the spaces as delimiters, thus creating a list of possible words.

F Now that I have all the possible words, I need to determine if the word fits our definition of a possible Proper Name. My rules here are simple, the length of the word must be greater than or equal *MIN_WORD*, less than or equal to *MAX_WORD* and must be in title case. Python provides a method associated with strings *istitle()* which returns *True* if the word is in title case and *False* if not.

G For each word that evaluates as a possible Proper Name, I add them to a Python dictionary. Python dictionaries are key/value pairs much like a physical dictionary. In this case the key will be the possible Proper Name and the value will be the number of occurrences of that Proper Name in the text.

H The Autopsy Report Class has a set of defined functions such as *getName*, *getDescription*, and *getRelativeFilePath*.

These functions provide key information to both our script and Autopsy. For example, the *getName* function identifies the specific report name that will be displayed in Autopsy for selection.

I Continuing with the function definitions of the Autopsy Report Class, the *generateReport()* method is where the custom report code is inserted. The first step is to obtain the list of available files from Autopsy using the *sleuth-kitCase.findAllFiles()* method. This returns a Python list object that contains the addressable file names held in the case. Next, the progress indicator in Autopsy is initialized in order to provide progress indication for the user. The next section will be setting up to read the contents of each file. *Note*: I have broken down the *generateReport()* method into several Sections I–M.

J This section creates a loop to process each filename that is included in the list of files returned from the *sleuthkitCase.findAllFiles()* method. Next, I'm going to target files that end with the.txt extension for this example to limit the Proper Name processing to just.txt file types. (*Note*: you can of course process any file within the case set not just.txt files.) Next, an input stream is setup to buffer the contents of the file as it is read from Autopsy; the buffer size is 1024 byte chunks in this example.

K In this step, the contents of the current file are read via the stream creating the *fileStringBuffer* in Python. This buffer is then passed to the *ExtractProperNames()* function as defined in Sections D–G. The result from the *ExtractProperNames()* function is a dictionary that contains each Proper Name along with the count or number of occurrences of each word found in the text.

L Once the file has been processed, the results need to be written to the report file. For each file processed, a header is created to separate the results and then each Proper Name along with number of occurrences is written to the report file. The report is sorted by the highest occurring words first.

M Finally, once all the files have been processed, the report file is closed, the process indicator is set to completed status, and the report is added to Autopsy.

Executing the Proper Names Script

Now that the walk-through of the code is completed, all that is left is to execute the Proper Names script from within Autopsy. To do this, we first copy the completed Python script to the appropriate Autopsy folder. In my case, the folder is shown in Fig. 6.8.

FIG. 6.8 Autopsy Python script module location.

Once the complete script has been copied to the Autopsy folder, we can launch Autopsy and utilize the script. Fig. 6.9 depicts the selection of the Proper Names script from the Generate Report menu option. Note the name of the report is *Proper Names Report* this report name was defined in the *generate-Report class* defined in Section H.

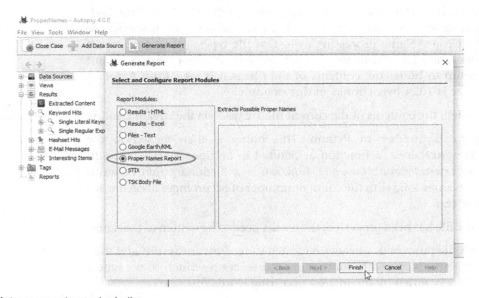

FIG. 6.9 Autopsy generate report selection.

Once the script is completed, the progress indicator and completion status are depicted in Fig. 6.10.

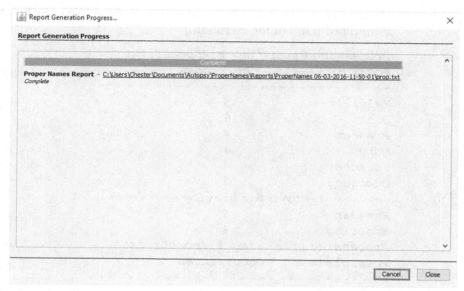

FIG. 6.10 Autopsy Report Generation completed.

The final report is then stored in the Reports section of Autopsy as shown in Fig. 6.11.

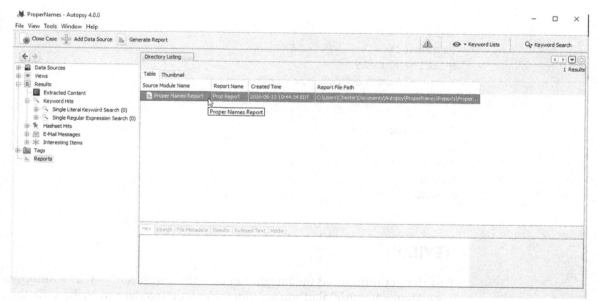

FIG. 6.11 Autopsy Report Generation completed.

The report output can now be viewed as shown here. (*Note*: the following is an abbreviated result of the execution.)

```
Processing File: /img_E:/Book02.txt
Possible Name    Occurrences
- - - - - - - - - - - - - - - - - - - - - - - - - - - - - -
Melville            5
Dick                5
Project             4
Moby                4
Gutenberg           4
Queequeg            3
~~~~~~ removed for brevity ~~~~~~~
Ramadan             1
Entering            1
Processing File: /img_E:/book01.txt
Possible Name    Occurrences
- - - - - - - - - - - - - - - - - - - - - - - - - - - - - -
Huck               84
Well               49
Potter             36
Aunt               34
Becky              34
Polly              33
Injun              33
Mary               26
Presently          25
Huckleberry25
~~~~~ Removed for brevity ~~~~~
Mister              1
Mayn                1
Salvation           1
Luck                1
Total               1
Clods               1
Shucks              1
```

REVIEW

This chapter introduced the integration of Python with Autopsy. The Autopsy open source forensic platform provides a unique interface to Python via the combination of Java and Sleuth Kit imported modules. Once the standard template was established, adding our own Python script to process the contents of an Autopsy case proved to be straightforward.

In addition to the overall `pyProper.py` script, the core function `ExtractProperNames()` was introduced that utilized several built-in Python string functions to extract the possible Proper Names from the selected files.

CHALLENGE PROBLEMS

(1) Modify the `pyProper.py` script to be used as an Autopsy Ingest module rather than a Report.
(2) Add the capability to the `pyProper.py` script to additionally sort the output alphabetically.
(3) Use the `pyProper.py script` as a baseline to develop your own addition to Autopsy.

Additional Resources

[1] Python-Tutorial One, http://www.basistech.com/python-autopsy-module-tutorial-1-the-file-ingest-module/.

[2] Python-Tutorial Two, http://www.basistech.com/python-autopsy-module-tutorial-2-the-data-source-ingest-module/.

[3] Python-Tutorial Three, http://www.basistech.com/python-autopsy-module-tutorial-3-the-report-module/.

[4] Autopsy Home Page, http://www.autopsy.com/.

## CHAPTER 7

Future Look and an Integration Challenge Problem

THE FUTURE

When I first wrote the book *"Python Forensics: A Workbench for Inventing and Sharing Digital Forensic Technology"* (ISBN: 978-0124186767) in 2014, there were literally no conference sessions or presentations discussing the use of Python in the field of digital investigation. Since then I have presented this work at dozens of conferences, training sessions, and webinars as well as in private settings. Also, virtually every cyber security or digital forensics conference has sessions that demonstrate how Python can enhance investigations, incident response methods, network monitoring, and general cyber security tools.

As you have seen in this book, many of the core tool makers and innovators are providing connectivity to Python within their tool sets. Developers and investigators are beginning to see the value of extending the capabilities of these platforms with their own unique innovations.

Graduate programs in digital forensics such as the Champlain College "Digital Forensic Science" Master Degree program have a required course in scripting that heavily relies on Python as the language of choice.

By integrating Python into existing proven platforms, we eliminate the need to reinvent the wheel and instead focus our script development on solving key challenges of the day. Then, we can include the results from these scripts into the overall case data. In addition, we can begin to develop new innovations that go far beyond acquisition, format, and display and provide real analytics (actually on a case by case basis), to the field of digital investigation.

As we move forward, I see the development of new innovations that examine information across cases, geographies, and even country boundaries. The application of reasoning technologies that extracted key evidence that was previously missed, providing correlations between victims, suspects, locations, timing, and organizations that were not before realized.

Integrating Python with Leading Computer Forensics Platforms. http://dx.doi.org/10.1016/B978-0-12-809949-0.00007-8

New techniques will take a harder look at certain file types that may contain valuable data or those that can include hidden content that would be valuable to an investigation. In 2012, I collaborated with Mike Raggo to write *"Data Hiding: Exposing Concealed Data in Multimedia, Operating Systems, Mobile Devices, and Network Protocols"* (ISBN: 978-1597497435). The book provided a broad look at the tools, techniques, and mitigation methods related to data hiding in traditional data hiding applications, mobile data hiding applications, network protocols, covert communication applications, as well as the operating system-based cloaking of data.

For the final Python script, I introduce a solution that extracts and unwinds information from the MP3 ID3 header. The script is not integrated into any of the Forensic Platforms that I have covered in this book. However, the script can easily be integrated into any one or all of the platforms. The task of performing the integration will be the challenge I leave you with.

Challenge Problem pyMP3.py

MP3 is an audio encoding format that employs lossy compression to reduce size with minimal impact on quality. The resulting MP3 content can be used to store files or to stream content over the Internet. MP3 is more formally referred to as MPEG-1 and MPEG-2 Audio Layer III and is governed by the **Moving Picture Experts Group (MPEG)**. MPEG was established by the International Standards Organization along with the International Electrotechnical Commission. The group's main goal is to establish standards for video and audio compression and distribution.

MP3 has become one of the most popular standards for the distribution of digital music files and is utilized by many popular streaming and file-based distribution services.

What Makes MP3 Attractive for Data Hiding?

The ubiquitous use of MP3 to share songs ultimately creates a large haystack of files and constant streaming content that makes it difficult to distinguish between benign vs infected sources. In addition, the header of the MP3 file can contain voluminous content that facilitates both simple and sophisticated data hiding layers. The simple depiction of the header as shown in Fig. 7.1 provides great value to audio enthusiasts to help manage, categorize, and dive deeper into the music that they enjoy.

Here is just a sampling of the ID3 Frames and associated tags that are available for encoding information within the ID3 Header.

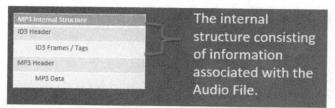

FIG. 7.1 Overview of the MP3 header.

'Audio encryption'
'Attached picture'
'Comments'
'Commercial frame'
'Encryption registration'
'Equalization'
'Event timing codes'
'General object'
'Group registration'
'Involved people list'
'Linked information'
'Music CD identifier'
'MPEG location lookup'
'Ownership frame'
'Play counter'
'Popularity meter'
'Position synchronization'
'Recommended buffer size'
'Relative volume adjustment'
'Reverb'
'Synchronized lyric/text'
'Synchronized tempo codes'
'Album/movie/show title'
'BPM beats per minute'
'Composer'
'Content type'
'Copyright message'
'Date'
'Playlist delay'
'Encoded by'
'Lyricist/text writer'
'File type'
'Time'
'Content group description'
'Title/songname/content description'
'Subtitle/Description refinement'
'Initial key'
'Language'
'Length'
'Media type'
'Original album/movie/show title'

```
'Original filename'
'Original lyricist/text writer'
'Original artist/performer'
'Original release year'
'File owner/licensee'
'Official webpage'
'Lead performer/soloist'
'Band/orchestra/accompaniment'
'Conductor/performer refinement'
'Interpreted, remixed, or otherwise modified by'
'Part of a set'
'Publisher'
'Track number/position in set'
'Recording dates'
'Internet radio station name'
'Internet radio station owner'
'International standard recording code'
'Software/hardware and settings used for encoding'
'User defined text information frame'
'UFID': 'Unique file identifier'
'USER': 'Terms of use'
'Unsychronized lyric/text transcription'
'Commercial information'
'Copyright/legal information'
'WOAF': 'Official audio file webpage'
'Official artist/performer webpage'
'WOAS': 'Official audio source webpage'
'WORS': 'Official internet radio station homepage'
'WPAY': 'Payment'
'WPUB': 'Publishers'
```

Even the novice data hider could see the value of embedding a variety of information into these innocuous fields. One simple example would be the use of the web-based data to fields to point to command and control locations. Or, the embedding of album cover art, band member photos, concert images, etc., to hide contraband or covert messages inside these seemingly benign and relevant images.

The following table shows sample data hiding methods along with an analysis of their complexity (Table 7.1).

To attack our challenge problem, the first step is to develop a Python script that extracts and analyzes the data contained with the ID3 fields and tags in order to assess the efficacy of the information included. The following script is well documented and as mentioned earlier can be executed standalone or easily integrated into the forensic platforms covered in this book; once again this is your challenge problem.

Table 7.1 Sample data hiding methods and analysis

Data hiding methods	Complexity of data hiding	Complexity of investigation
Blending text-based content into existing tags	Easy	Moderate
Using date tags to communicate events	Easy	Difficult
Communicating contacts and associates using fields reserved for artists, composers, and publishers	Moderate	Difficult
Hiding information in the available PAD areas of the ID3	Moderate	Difficult
Leveraging URL tags to communicate CNC or web-based resources	Moderate	Difficult
Embedding relevant images that contain hidden content	Moderate	Hard
Embedding encrypted text or null ciphers	Moderate	Hard

pyMP3.py Python Script

```
'''

MP3-ID3Forensics

Python Script (with no 3rd party modules)
For the extraction of meta data and
potential evidence hidden in MP3 files
specifically in the ID3 Headers

Author C. Hosmer
        Python Forensics

Copyright (c) 2015-2016 Chet Hosmer / Python Forensics, Inc.

Permission is hereby granted, free of charge, to any person obtaining a copy
of this software and associated documentation files (the "Software"), to deal
in the Software without restriction, including without limitation the rights
to use, copy, modify, merge, publish, distribute, sublicense, and/or sell
copies of the Software, and to permit persons to whom the Software is
furnished to do so, subject to the following conditions:

The above copyright notice and this permission notice shall be included in all
copies or substantial portions of the Software.

'''

# IMPORT MODULES

# Standard Python Libraries

import os                          # Standard Operating System Methods
import argparse                    # Command Line Argument Parsing
```

```python
from struct import *          # Handle Strings as Binary Data
import string                 # Special string Module
import time                   # Date Time Module

# Function: GetTime()
#
# Returns a string containing the current time
#
# Script will use the local system clock, time, date and timezone
# to calcuate the current time. Thus you should sync your system
# clock before using this script
#
# Input: timeStyle = 'UTC', 'LOCAL', the function will default to
#                    UTC Time if you pass in nothing.

def GetTime(timeStyle = "UTC"):

    if timeStyle == 'UTC':
        return ('UTC Time: ', time.asctime(time.gmtime(time.time())))
    else:
        return ('LOC Time: ', time.asctime(time.localtime(time.time())))

# End GetTime Function =============================


#
# Print Hexidecimal / ASCII Page Heading
#

def PrintHeading():

    print("Offset        00 01 02 03 04 05 06 07 08 09 0A 0B 0C
0D 0E 0F        ASCII")
    print("--------------------------------------------------------------
---------------------------")

    return

# End PrintHeading

#
# Print ID3 Frame Contents
#
# Input: buff - Holding the frame content
#        buffSize - Size of the frame contents
#

def PrintContents(buff, buffSize):
```

```
        PrintHeading()
        offset = 0

        # Loop through 1 line at a time

        for i in range(offset, offset+buffSize, 16):

            # Print the current offset

            print "%08x   " % i,

            # Print 16 Hex Bytes
            for j in range(0,16):
                if i+j >= buffSize:
                    print ' ',
                else:
                    byteValue = ord(buff[i+j])
                    print "%02x " % byteValue,
            print "   ",

            # Print 16 Ascii equivelents

            for j in range (0,16):
                if i+j >= buffSize:
                    break
                byteValue = ord(buff[i+j])
                # If printable characters print them
                if (byteValue >= 0x20 and byteValue <= 0x7f):
                    print "%c" % byteValue,
                else:
                    print '.',
            print

        return

# End Print Buffer
'''
ID3 Class

Extracting Meta and Evidence from mp3 files
'''

class ID3():

#Class Constructor

    def __init__(self, theFile):

        # Initialize Attributes of the Object
```

```
# Local Constants

self.KNOWN_TAGS_V3 = {
    'AENC': 'Audio encryption:                          ',
    'APIC': 'Attached picture:                          ',
    'COMM': 'Comments:                                  ',
    'COMR': 'Commercial frame:                          ',
    'ENCR': 'Encryption method registration:   ',
    'EQUA': 'Equalization:                              ',
    'ETCO': 'Event timing codes:                        ',
    'GEOB': 'General encapsulated object:        ',
    'GRID': 'Grp identification registration: ',
    'IPLS': 'Involved people list:                  ',
    'LINK': 'Linked information:                        ',
    'MCDI': 'Music CD identifier:                       ',
    'MLLT': 'MPEG location lookup table:         ',
    'OWNE': 'Ownership frame:                           ',
    'PRIV': 'Private frame:                             ',
    'PCNT': 'Play counter:                              ',
    'POPM': 'Popularimeter:                             ',
    'POSS': 'Position synchronisation frame:   ',
    'RBUF': 'Recommended buffer size:               ',
    'RGAD': 'Replay Gain Adjustment:                ',
    'RVAD': 'Relative volume adjustment:         ',
    'RVRB': 'Reverb:                                    ',
    'SYLT': 'Synchronized lyric/text:             ',
    'SYTC': 'Synchronized tempo codes:            ',
    'TALB': 'Album/Movie/Show title:                ',
    'TBPM': 'BPM beats per minute:                  ',
    'TCOM': 'Composer:                                  ',
    'TCON': 'Content type:                              ',
    'TCOP': 'Copyright message:                         ',
    'TDAT': 'Date:                                      ',
    'TDLY': 'Playlist delay:                            ',
    'TDRC': 'Recording Time:                            ',
    'TENC': 'Encoded by:                                ',
    'TEXT': 'Lyricist/Text writer:                  ',
    'TFLT': 'File type:                                 ',
    'TIME': 'Time:                                      ',
    'TIT1': 'Content group description:             ',
    'TIT2': 'Title/songname/content descrip:  ',
    'TIT3': 'Subtitle/Description refinement: ',
    'TKEY': 'Initial key:                               ',
    'TLAN': 'Language:                                  ',
```

```
            'TLEN': 'Length:                              ',
            'TMED': 'Media type:                          ',
            'TOAL': 'Original album/movie/show title:     ',
            'TOFN': 'Original filename:                   ',
            'TOLY': 'Original lyricist/text writer:       ',
            'TOPE': 'Original artist/performer:           ',
            'TORY': 'Original release year:               ',
            'TOWN': 'File owner/licensee:                 ',
            'TPE1': 'Lead performer/Soloist:              ',
            'TPE2': 'Band/orchestra/accompaniment:        ',
            'TPE3': 'Conductor/performer refinement:      ',
            'TPE4': 'Interpreted, remixed, modified by:   ',
            'TPOS': 'Part of a set:                       ',
            'TPUB': 'Publisher:                           ',
            'TRCK': 'Track number/Position in set:        ',
            'TRDA': 'Recording dates:                     ',
            'TRSN': 'Internet radio station name:         ',
            'TRSO': 'Internet radio station owner:        ',
            'TSIZ': 'Size:                                ',
            'TSRC': 'Intl standard recording code:        ',
            'TSSE': 'SW/HW settings used for encoding:    ',
            'TYER': 'User defined text frame:             ',
            'TXXX': 'User define general text frame:      ',
            'UFID': 'Unique file identifier:              ',
            'USER': 'Terms of use:                        ',
            'USLT': 'Unsyched lyric/text transcription:',
            'WCOM': 'Commercial information:              ',
            'WCOP': 'Copyright/Legal informationL         ',
            'WOAF': 'Official audio file webpage:         ',
            'WOAR': 'Official artist/performer webpage:',
            'WOAS': 'Official audio source webpage:       ',
            'WORS': 'Official internet radio homepage:    ',
            'WPAY': 'Payment:                             ',
            'WPUB': 'Publishers official webpage:         ',
            'WXXX': 'User defined URL link frame:         '
            }

    self.KNOWN_TAGS_V2 = {
        'BUF': 'Recommended buffer size',
        'COM': 'Comments',
        'CNT': 'Play counter',
        'CRA': 'Audio Encryption',
        'CRM': 'Encrypted meta frame',
        'ETC': 'Event timing codes',
```

```
'EQU': 'Equalization',
'GEO': 'General encapsulated object',
'IPL': 'Involved people list',
'LNK': 'Linked information',
'MCI': 'Music CD Identifier',
'MLL': 'MPEG location lookup table',
'PIC': 'Attached picture',
'POP': 'Popularimeter',
'REV': 'Reverb',
'RVA': 'Relative volume adjustment',
'SLT': 'Synchronized lyric/text',
'STC': 'Synced tempo codes',
'TAL': 'Album/Movie/Show title',
'TBP': 'BPM Beats Per Minute',
'TCM': 'Composer',
'TCO': 'Content type',
'TCR': 'Copyright message',
'TDA': 'Date',
'TDY': 'Playlist delay',
'TEN': 'Encoded by',
'TFT': 'File type',
'TIM': 'Time',
'TKE': 'Initial key',
'TLA': 'Languages',
'TLE': 'Length',
'TMT': 'Media type',
'TOA': 'Original artists/performers',
'TOF': 'Original filename',
'TOL': 'Original Lyricists/text writers',
'TOR': 'Original release year',
'TOT': 'Original album/Movie/Show title',
'TP1': 'Lead  artist(s)/Lead  performer(s)/Soloist(s)/Performing
group',
'TP2': 'Band/Orchestra/Accompaniment',
'TP3': 'Conductor/Performer refinement',
'TP4': 'Interpreted, remixed, or otherwise modified by',
'TPA': 'Part of a set',
'TPB': 'Publisher',
'TRC': 'International Standard Recording Code',
'TRD': 'Recording dates',
'TRK': 'Track number/Position in set',
'TSI': 'Size',
'TSS': 'Software/hardware and settings used for encoding',
'TT1': 'Content group description',
```

```python
        'TT2': 'Title/Songname/Content description',
        'TT3': 'Subtitle/Description refinement',
        'TXT': 'Lyricist/text writer',
        'TXX': 'Year',
        'UFI': 'Unique file identifier',
        'ULT': 'Unsychronized lyric/text transcription',
        'WAF': 'Official audio file webpage',
        'WAR': 'Official artist/performer webpage',
        'WAS': 'Official audio source webpage',
        'WCM': 'Commercial information',
        'WCP': 'Copyright/Legal information',
        'WPB': 'Publishers official webpage',
        'WXX': 'User defined URL link frame'
    }

    self.picTypeList = [
                'Other',
                'fileIcon',
                'OtherIcon',
                'FrontCover',
                'BackCover',
                'LeafletPage',
                'Media',
                'LeadArtist',
                'ArtistPerformer',
                'Conductor',
                'BandOrchestra',
                'Composer',
                'Lyricist',
                'RecordingLocation',
                'DuringRecording',
                'DuringPerformance',
                'MovieScreenCapture',
                'Fish',
                'Illustration',
                'BandArtistLogo',
                'PublisherStudioLogo'
                ]

    # Attributes of the Class

    self.fileName     = ''
    self.id3Size      = 0
    self.fileContents = ''
```

```
self.mp3              = False
self.id3              = False

self.hdr              = ''
self.flag             = 0
self.version          = 0
self.revision         = 0

self.unsync           = False
self.extendedHeader   = False
self.experimental     = False

self.hasPicture       = False
self.imageCount       = 0

self.frameList        = []

self.padArea          = ''

# Now Process the Proposed MP3 File

try:
    self.fileName = theFile
    with open(theFile, 'rb') as mp3File:
        self.fileContents = mp3File.read()
except:
    print "Could not process input file: ", theFile
    quit()

#Strip off the first 10 characters of the file
stripHeader = self.fileContents[0:6]

#now unpack the header
id3Header = unpack('3sBBB', stripHeader)

self.hdr        = id3Header[0]
self.version    = id3Header[1]
self.revision   = id3Header[2]
self.flag       = id3Header[3]

if self.hdr == 'ID3' and self.version in range(2,4):
    self.id3 = True
else:
    self.id3 = False
    print "MP3 File type not supported"
    quit()

# If we seem to have a valid MP3 ID3 Header
# Attempt to Process the Header
```

```
        # Get Size Bytes and unpack them
        stripSize = self.fileContents[6:10]

        id3Size = unpack('BBBB', stripSize)

        # Calculate the Size (this is a bit tricky)
        # and add in the 10 byte header not included
        # in the size

        self.id3Size = self.calcID3Size(id3Size) + 10

        # check the unsync flag
        if self.flag & 0x60:
            self.unsync = True

        # check the extended header flag
        if self.flag & 0x40:
            self.extendedHeader = True

        # check the experimental indicator
        if self.flag & 0x40:
            self.experimental = True

        self.processID3Frames()

        return
    '''
    Print out any extracted header information
    '''

    def printResults(self):
        print "==== MP3/ID3 Header Information"
        print "ID3 Found:     ", self.id3

        if self.id3:
            print "File:              ", self.fileName
            print "ID3 Hdr Size:      ", self.hdr
            print "Version:           ", self.version
            print "Revision:          ", self.revision
            print "Size:              ", self.id3Size
            print "Unsync             ", self.unsync
            print "Extended Header:   ", self.extendedHeader
            print "Experimental:      ", self.experimental
            print "Images Found:      ", str(self.imageCount)
            print  "\n--------------------------------------------------
---------------"

            print "ID3 Frames"
```

```
            print     "---------------------------------------------------
---------------"

        for entry in self.frameList:
            print "FrameID:              ", entry[0]
            print "Frame Type:           ", entry[1]
            print "Frame Size:           ", entry[2]

            print "Tag Preservation:    ", entry[4]
            print "File Preservation:   ", entry[5]
            print "Read Only:           ", entry[6]
            print "Compressed:          ", entry[7]
            print "Encrypted:           ", entry[8]
            print "Group Identity:      ", entry[9]
            print "\nFrame Content:\n"
            PrintContents(entry[3], len(entry[3]))
            print
"==========================================================================
===========================\n"

        print "\nPad Area - Size", len(self.padArea)
        if len(self.padArea) != 0:
            PrintContents(self.padArea, len(self.padArea))

        print "\n\n END PyMP3 Forensics"

    def processID3Frames(self):

        if self.id3:

            # starting first frame location
            frameOffset = 10
            imageCount = 0

            # Loop Through all the frames until we reach
            # Null ID

            # while self.fileContents[frameOffset] != '\000':

            while frameOffset < self.id3Size:

                # check for padding
                if self.fileContents[frameOffset] == '\000':
                    # we are at the end of the frame
                    # and we have found padding
                    # record the pad area
                    self.padArea =
self.fileContents[frameOffset:self.id3Size]
                    break
```

```python
if self.version == 2:

    # Version 2 Headers contain
    # 6 bytes
    # sss = type
    # xxx = size

    frameID   =
self.fileContents[frameOffset:frameOffset+3]

    if frameID in self.KNOWN_TAGS_V2:
        frameDescription = self.KNOWN_TAGS_V2[frameID]
    else:
        frameDescription = 'Unknown'

    frameOffset +=3
    stripSize =
self.fileContents[frameOffset:frameOffset+3]
    frameOffset +=3
    frameSize = unpack('BBB', stripSize)

    integerFrameSize = self.calcFrameSize(frameSize)

    # If the frame is a picture
    # extract the contents of the picture and create
    # a separate file

    if frameID == "PIC":
        self.hasPicture = True
        # bump the image count in case multiple images
        # are included in this file
        self.imageCount+=1
        self.extractPicture(frameOffset, 2, integerFrameSize,
self.imageCount)
    # For version 2 set all version 3 flags to False
    tagPreservation  = False
    filePreservation = False
    readOnly         = False
    compressed       = False
    encrypted        = False
    groupID          = 0

elif self.version == 3:

    # Version 3 Headers contain
    # 10 Bytes
    # ssss = Type
```

```
# xxxx = size
# xx  = flags

v3Header = self.fileContents[frameOffset:frameOffset+10]
frameOffset += 10
try:
    frameHeader = unpack('!4sIBB', v3Header)
except:
    print "Unpack Failed"
    quit()

frameID          = frameHeader[0]
integerFrameSize = frameHeader[1]
flag1            = frameHeader[2]
flag2            = frameHeader[3]

if frameID == 'APIC':
    self.hasPicture = True
    # bump the image count in case multiple images
    # are included in this file
    self.imageCount+=1
    self.extractPicture(frameOffset, 3, integerFrameSize,
                        self.imageCount)

if frameID in self.KNOWN_TAGS_V3:
    frameDescription = self.KNOWN_TAGS_V3[frameID]
else:
    frameDescription = 'Unknown'

if flag1 & 0x80:
    tagPreservation = False
else:
    tagPreservation = True

if flag1 & 0x60:
    filePreservation = False
else:
    filePreservation = True

if flag1 & 0x40:
    readOnly = True
else:
    readOnly = False

if flag2 & 0x80:
    compressed = True
else:
    compressed = False
```

```
            if flag2 & 0x60:
                encrypted = True
            else:
                encrypted = False

            if flag2 & 0x40:
                groupId = True
            else:
                groupID = False
            else:
                print "Version Not Supported"
                quit()

            frameContent =
self.fileContents[frameOffset:frameOffset+integerFrameSize]
            frameOffset += integerFrameSize

            # Add frame information
            self.frameList.append([frameID, frameDescription,
integerFrameSize, frameContent, tagPreservation, filePreservation, readOnly,
compressed, encrypted, groupID])
            print frameID, frameDescription,

            if frameContent[0] == "\000":
                frameDump = frameContent[1:]
            else:
                frameDump = frameContent

            frameSnip = ''

            if frameID == "COMM":
                for eachChar in frameDump:
                    if eachChar in string.printable:
                        frameSnip = frameSnip + eachChar
                    else:
                        continue
            else:
                for eachChar in frameDump:
                    if eachChar in string.printable:
                        frameSnip = frameSnip + eachChar
                    else:
                        break
            print frameSnip[0:80]
            print
        return

    '''

    extractPicture from ID3 Frame
```

```
    input: offset to the frame
           version (2 or 3)

           writes output to an images directory
           note the images directory must exist
           ./images/

'''

def extractPicture(self, off, ver, lenOfFrame, imgCnt):

    if ver == 2:

        # Now extract the picture type
        picType = ''
        typeOffset = off+1

        while self.fileContents[typeOffset] != '\000':
            picType = picType+self.fileContents[typeOffset]
            typeOffset+=1

        # skip terminating characters

        while self.fileContents[typeOffset] == '\000':
            typeOffset+=1

        # Extract the picture from the content
        thePicture = self.fileContents[typeOffset:off+lenOfFrame]

        # Create a unique name each picture relating to the original
        # filename into a sub-directory named images

        imageName =
"./images/"+os.path.basename(self.fileName)+".image"+str(imgCnt)+"."+picType

        # Open the file for writing and write out the content
        with open(imageName, "wb") as out:
            out.write(thePicture)

    elif ver == 3:

            # Now extract the picture type
            mimeType = ''
            typeOffset = off+1

            while self.fileContents[typeOffset] != '\000':
                mimeType = mimeType+self.fileContents[typeOffset]
                typeOffset+=1

            # Set the file extension based on the mime type
            if mimeType.find('jpeg'):
```

```
                    ext = "jpg"
            elif mimeType.find('png'):
                    ext = "png"
            else:
                    ext = "dat"

            # skip terminating characters

            while self.fileContents[typeOffset] == '\000':
                    typeOffset+=1

            # Next Byte is the Picture Type
            picType = self.fileContents[typeOffset]
            intPicType = ord(picType)

            if intPicType >= 0 and intPicType <= len(self.picTypeList):
                    picTypeStr = self.picTypeList[intPicType]
            else:
                    picTypeStr = "Unknown"

            typeOffset += 1
            # skip terminating characters

            while self.fileContents[typeOffset] == '\000':
                    typeOffset+=1

            # Extract the picture from the content
            thePicture = self.fileContents[typeOffset:off+lenOfFrame]

            # Unique name for each picture relating to the original
            # filename into a sub-directory named images

            imageName =
"./images/"+os.path.basename(self.fileName)+'.'+picTypeStr+'.'+str(imgCnt)+".
"+ext

            # Open the file for writing and write out the content
            with open(imageName, "wb") as out:
                    out.write(thePicture)'
    '''
```

Calculate the ID3 Size

The ID3 Size is 28 bits spread over 4 bytes in Big Endian Format the MSB of each byte is ignored and the remaining 7 bits of each byte are concatenated together to produce a 28 bit string.

For example the four byte size shown below:

0x0 0x1 0x4a 0x3

Creates the following 28 bit string

0000000000000110010100000011

for a decimal integer value of:

25859

Adding in the 10 header bytes (which is not included in the size) the total size is:

25869

Excerpt from ID3 Standard

The ID3 tag size is the size of the complete tag after unsynchronisation, including padding, excluding the header (total tag size - 10). The reason to use 28 bits (representing up to 256MB) for size description is that we don't want to run out of space here.

calcID3Size (receives a tuple of the four bytes)

```
'''
def calcID3Size(self, bytes):
    # Convert the tuple to a list for easy processing

    bytes = list(bytes)

    # Ensure that the MSB of each Byte is zero

    bytes[0] = bytes[0] & 0x7f
    bytes[1] = bytes[1] & 0x7f
    bytes[2] = bytes[2] & 0x7f
    bytes[3] = bytes[3] & 0x7f

    # Initialize the bit string we will create
    bits = ""

    # loop through each byte setting each
    # to a '1' or '0' starting with bit 6

    for val in bytes:

        i = 64

        # continue until we process all bits
        # from bit 6-0

        while i > 0:
            if val & i:
                bits = bits + '1'
            else:
                bits = bits + '0'

            # move to the next lower bit
```

```
         i = i/2

    # Now simply Convert the Binary String to an Integer

    integerSize = int(bits,2)

    return integerSize
'''
Calculate the Frame size from the 3 hex bytes provided

Excerpt from ID3v2 Standard

    The three character frame identifier is followed by a three byte size
    descriptor, making a total header size of six bytes in every frame.
    The size is calculated as framesize excluding frame identifier and
    size descriptor (frame size - 6).

calcFrameSize (receives a tuple of the three bytes)
'''
def calcFrameSize(self, bytes):

    valList = list(bytes)

    finalValue = valList[0] << 16
    finalValue = finalValue | valList[1] << 8
    finalValue = finalValue | valList[2]

    return finalValue

'''
Main Program
'''
def main():
    print
    print "Python Forensics, Inc. www.python-forensics.org"
    print "Python MP3 Forensics v 1.0 June 2016"
    print "developed by: C. Hosmer"
    print
    print "Script Started", GetTime()
    print

    # Process the command line arguments

    parser = argparse.ArgumentParser()
    parser.add_argument('mp3File')
    theArgs = parser.parse_args()

    # Obtain the single argument which is the
    # full path name of the file to process
```

```
    mp3File = theArgs.mp3File

    # set the output to verbose
    verbose = True

    print "Processing MP3 File: ", mp3File
    print

    # Process the mp3File
    objID3 = ID3 (mp3File)

    # If verbose is selected the print results to standard out
    # otherwise create a log file

    if objID3.id3:
        if verbose:
            objID3.printResults()
        else:
            # Turn on Logging

logging.basicConfig(filename='pSearchLog.log',level=logging.DEBUG,
format='%(asctime)s %(message)s')
                objID3.logResults()
if __name__ == "__main__":
    main()
```

Executing pyMP3.py

To execute the script as is, before integrating it into a forensic platform, you first need to setup a simple folder structure as shown here in Fig. 7.2.

As you can see, the pyMP3.py file and the images folder are required. The sample .mp3 files can exist anywhere; however, I decided to place them in the same folder for easy access. This way the running of the script from the command line is simple. For example, navigate to the appropriate folder and then type: **python pyMP3.py EO.mp3**

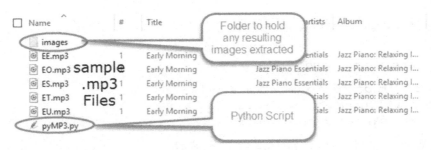

FIG. 7.2 Folder structure pyMP3.py.

The abbreviated output is shown here:

```
Python Forensics, Inc. www.python-forensics.org
Python MP3 Forensics v 1.0 June 2016
developed by: C. Hosmer

Script Started ('UTC Time: ', 'Tue Jun 14 15:50:00 2016')

Processing MP3 File: EE.mp3

PRIV Private frame:                        www.amazon.com

TPE1 Lead performer/Soloist:               Jazz Piano Essentials

TALB Album/Movie/Show title:               Jazz Piano: Relaxing Instrumental
Music, Best Background Dinner Music Solo Piano

TPE2 Band/orchestra/accompaniment:         Jazz Piano Essentials

TIT2 Title/songname/content descrip:       Early Morning

TCOP Copyright message:                    2010 Real Jazz Records

TPUB Publisher:                            Rftolynp Dzqehlcp

TRCK Track number/Position in set:         1/27

TPOS Part of a set:                        1/1

TSSE SW/HW settings used for encoding:     11

TYER User defined text frame:              2010

TDRC Recording Time:                       2010

RGAD Replay Gain Adjustment:

TXXX User define general text frame:       replaygain_track_gain

COMM Comments:                             XXXAmazon.com Song ID: 219962720

TCON Content type:                         Jazz

APIC Attached picture:                     image/jpeg
```

```
APIC Attached picture:    image/jpeg
APIC Attached picture:    image/jpeg

=== MP3/ID3 Header Information
ID3 Found:        True
File:             EE.mp3
ID3 Hdr Size:     ID3
Version:          3
Revision:         0
Size:             231895
Unsync            False
Extended Header:  False
Experimental:     False
Images Found:     3

-------------------------------------
ID3 Frames
-------------------------------------
FrameID: PRIV
Frame Type:        Private frame:
Frame Size:        8207
Tag Preservation:  True
File Preservation: True
Read Only:         False
Compressed:        False
Encrypted:         False
Group Identity:    False

Frame Content:

-------------------------------------
Offset    00 01 02 03 04 05 06 07 08 09 0A 0B 0C 0D 0E 0F
ASCII
-------------------------------------
00000000  77 77 77 2e 61 6d 61 7a 6f 6e 2e 63 6f 6d 00 00
www.amazon.com..
00000010  00 00 00 00 00 00 00 00 00 00 00 00 00 00 00 00
..............
```

```
00000020  00 00 00 00 00 00 00 00 00 00 00 00 00 00 00 00  ................
00000030  00 00 00 00 00 00 00 00 00 00 00 00 00 00 00 00  ................
00000040  00 00 00 00 00 00 00 00 00 00 00 00 00 00 00 00  ................
          ~~~~~~~ Cut for Brevity ~~~~~~~
00001ff0  00 00 00 00 00 00 00 00 00 00 00 00 00 00 00 00  ................
00002000  00 00 00 00 00 00 00 00 00 00 00 00 00 00 00 00  ................
          ................
=================================
=================================

FrameID: TPE1
Frame Type:         Lead performer/Soloist:
Frame Size:         22
Tag Preservation:   True
File Preservation:  True
Read Only:          False
Compressed:         False
Encrypted:          False
Group Identity:     False

Frame Content:

Offset   00 01 02 03 04 05 06 07 08 09 0A 0B 0C 0D 0E 0F
ASCII
---------------------------------
00000000  00 4a 61 7a 7a 20 50 69 61 6e 6f 20 45 73 73 65
          .Jazz Piano Esse
00000010  6e 74 69 61 6c 73
          ntials
=================================
=================================
```

```
FrameID: TALB
Frame Type:          Album/Movie/Show title:
Frame Size:          100
Tag Preservation:    True
File Preservation:   True
Read Only:           False
Compressed:          False
Encrypted:           False
Group Identity:      False

Frame Content:

Offset   00 01 02 03 04 05 06 07 08 09 0A 0B 0C 0D 0E 0F
ASCII
------------------------------------------------------------
00000000 00 4a 61 7a 7a 20 50 69 61 6e 6f 3a 20 52 65 6c
.Jazz Piano:   Rel
00000010 61 78 69 6e 67 20 49 6e 73 74 72 75 6d 65 6e 74
axing Instrument
00000020 61 6c 20 4d 75 73 69 63 2c 20 42 65 73 74 20 42
al Music, Best B
00000030 61 63 6b 67 72 6f 75 6e 64 20 44 69 6e 6e 65 72
ackground Dinner
00000040 20 4d 75 73 69 63 20 53 6f 6c 6f 20 50 69 61 6e
 Music Solo Pian
00000050 6f 20 45 73 73 65 6e 74 69 61 6c 73 20 45 64 69
o Essentials Edi
00000060 74 69 6f 6e
tion
============================================
============================================

FrameID: TPE2
Frame Type:          Band/orchestra/accompaniment:
Frame Size:          22
Tag Preservation:    True
File Preservation:   True
```

Read Only: False
Compressed: False
Encrypted: False
Group Identity: False

Frame Content:

```
Offset    00  01  02  03  04  05  06  07  08  09  0A  0B  0C  0D  0E  0F
ASCII
---------------------------------------------------------------------------
00000000  00  4a  61  7a  7a  20  50  69  61  6e  6f  20  45  73  73  65
          . J  a  z  z     P  i  a  n  o     E  s  s  e
00000010  6e  74  69  61  6c  73
          n  t  i  a  l  s
===========================================================================
===========================================================================
```

FrameID: TIT2
Frame Type: Title/songname/content descrip:
Frame Size: 14
Tag Preservation: True
File Preservation: True
Read Only: False
Compressed: False
Encrypted: False
Group Identity: False

Frame Content:

```
Offset    00  01  02  03  04  05  06  07  08  09  0A  0B  0C  0D  0E  0F
ASCII
---------------------------------------------------------------------------
00000000  00  45  61  72  6c  79  20  4d  6f  72  6e  69  6e  67
          . E  a  r  l  y     M  o  r  n  i  n  g
===========================================================================
===========================================================================
```

```
FrameID: TCOP
Frame Type:          Copyright message:
Frame Size:          23
Tag Preservation:    True
File Preservation:   True
Read Only:           False
Compressed:          False
Encrypted:           False
Group Identity:      False

Frame Content:

Offset   00  01  02  03  04  05  06  07  08  09  0A  0B  0C  0D  0E  0F
ASCII
------------------------------------------------------------------------
00000000 00  32  30  31  30  20  52  65  61  6c  20  4a  61  7a  7a  20
         .2010 Real Jazz
00000010 52  65  63  6f  72  64  73
         Records
========================================
========================================

FrameID: TPUB
Frame Type:          Publisher:
Frame Size:          18
Tag Preservation:    True
File Preservation:   True
Read Only:           False
Compressed:          False
Encrypted:           False
Group Identity:      False

Frame Content:

Offset   00  01  02  03  04  05  06  07  08  09  0A  0B  0C  0D  0E  0F
ASCII
------------------------------------------------------------------------
```

```
00000000  00  52  66  74  6f  6c  79  6e  70  20  44  7a  71  65  68  6c
.R f t o l y n p   D z q e h l
00000010  63  70
c p
================================================================
================================

FrameID: TRCK
Frame Type:            Track number/Position in set:
Frame Size:            5
Tag Preservation:      True
File Preservation:     True
Read Only:             False
Compressed:            False
Encrypted:             False
Group Identity:        False

Frame Content:

Offset  00  01  02  03  04  05  06  07  08  09  0A  0B  0C  0D  0E  0F
ASCII

----------------------------------------------------------------

00000000  00  31  2f 32  37
. 1 / 2 7
================================================================
==========================

FrameID: TPOS
Frame Type:            Part of a set:
Frame Size:            4
Tag Preservation:      True
File Preservation:     True
Read Only:             False
Compressed:            False
Encrypted:             False
Group Identity:        False

Frame Content:
```

```
Offset     00  01  02  03  04  05  06  07  08  09  0A  0B  0C  0D  0E  0F
ASCII
-------------------------------------------------------------------------
00000000   00  31  2f  31
.1/1
=========================================================================
=========================================================================

FrameID: TSSE
Frame Type:          SW/HW settings used for encoding:
Frame Size:          3
Tag Preservation:    True
File Preservation:   True
Read Only:           False
Compressed:          False
Encrypted:           False
Group Identity:      False

Frame Content:

Offset     00  01  02  03  04  05  06  07  08  09  0A  0B  0C  0D  0E  0F
ASCII
-------------------------------------------------------------------------
00000000   00  31  31
.11
=========================================================================
=========================================================================

FrameID: TYER
Frame Type:          User defined text frame:
Frame Size:          5
Tag Preservation:    True
File Preservation:   True
Read Only:           False
Compressed:          False
Encrypted:           False
Group Identity:      False
```

Frame Content:

```
Offset     00   01   02   03   04   05   06   07   08   09   0A   0B   0C   0D   0E   0F
ASCII
-----------------------------------------------------------------------------------------
00000000   00   32   30   31   30
.2010
=========================================================================================
```

FrameID: TDRC

Frame Type: Recording Time:
Frame Size: 5
Tag Preservation: True
File Preservation: True
Read Only: False
Compressed: False
Encrypted: False
Group Identity: False

Frame Content:

```
Offset     00   01   02   03   04   05   06   07   08   09   0A   0B   0C   0D   0E   0F
ASCII
-----------------------------------------------------------------------------------------
00000000   00   32   30   31   30
.2010
=========================================================================================
```

FrameID: RGAD

Frame Type: Replay Gain Adjustment:
Frame Size: 8
Tag Preservation: True
File Preservation: False
Read Only: True
Compressed: False
Encrypted: False
Group Identity: False

Frame Content:

```
Offset     00   01   02   03   04   05   06   07   08   09   0A   0B   0C   0D   0E   0F
ASCII
------------------------------------------------------------------------------------------
00000000   bf   80   00   00   2e   2c   00   00
. . . . . , ,
==========================================
```

FrameID: TXXX
Frame Type: *User define general text frame:*
Frame Size: 31
Tag Preservation: True
File Preservation: True
Read Only: False
Compressed: False
Encrypted: False
Group Identity: False

Frame Content:

```
Offset     00   01   02   03   04   05   06   07   08   09   0A   0B   0C   0D   0E   0F
ASCII
------------------------------------------------------------------------------------------
00000000   00   72   65   70   6c   61   79   67   61   69   6e   5f   74   72   61   63
. r  e  p  l  a  y  g  a  i  n  _  t  r  a  c
00000010   6b   5f   67   61   69   6e   00   2d   34   2e   34   30   20   64   42
k _ g a i n . - 4 . 4 0 d B
==========================================
```

FrameID: COMM
Frame Type: *Comments:*
Frame Size: 34
Tag Preservation: True
File Preservation: True
Read Only: False

Compressed: False
Encrypted: False
Group Identity: False

Frame Content:

```
Offset    00  01  02  03  04  05  06  07  08  09  0A  0B  0C  0D  0E  0F
ASCII
---------------------------------------------------------------------------
00000000  00  58  58  58  00  41  6d  61  7a  6f  6e  2e  63  6f  6d  20
.XXX.Amazon.com
00000010  53  6f  6e  67  20  49  44  3a  20  32  31  39  39  36  32  37
Song  ID: 2199627
00000020  32  30
2 0
```
==============================
==============================

FrameID: TCON
Frame Type: Content type:
Frame Size: 5
Tag Preservation: True
File Preservation: True
Read Only: False
Compressed: False
Encrypted: False
Group Identity: False

Frame Content:

```
Offset    00  01  02  03  04  05  06  07  08  09  0A  0B  0C  0D  0E  0F
ASCII
---------------------------------------------------------------------------
00000000  00  4a  61  7a  7a
.Jazz
```

```
================================================
================================

FrameID: APIC
Frame Type:            Attached picture:
Frame Size:            171845
Tag Preservation:      True
File Preservation:     True
Read Only:             False
Compressed:            False
Encrypted:             False
Group Identity:        False

Frame Content:

Offset    00   01   02   03   04   05   06   07   08   09   0A   0B   0C   0D   0E   0F
ASCII

------------------------------------------------
------

00000000  00   69   6d   61   67   65   2f   6a   70   65   67   00   03   00   ff   d8
.image/jpeg.....
00000010  ff   e0   00   10   4a 46   49   46   00   01   01   00   00   01   00   01
....JFIF......
00000020  00   00   ff   db   00   43   00   01   01   01   01   01   01   01   01   01
.....C..........
00000030  01   01   01   01   01   01   01   01   01   01   01   01   01   01   01   01
................
~~~~~~~~~~~ Cut  for  Brevity ~~~~~~~~~~
00029f20  39   c7   f9   ed   fe   45   14   53   72   6f   76   c0   90   48   c0   82
9....E.Srov..H..
00029f30  37   67   23   3d   46   3a   73   9c   75   f7   1f   9d   14   51   48   4e
7 g#=F:s.u...QHN
00029f40  29   ea   d1   ff   d9
)....
================================================
================================

END PyMP3 Forensics
```

EE.mp3.BackCover.2.jpg

EE.mp3.FrontCover.1.jpg

EE.mp3.LeadArtist.3.jpg

FIG. 7.3 Resulting ./images/ folder.

Examining the output folder *./images/*, you see the thumbnails of the images that were carved from the .mp3 ID3 header in Fig. 7.3.

REVIEW

This chapter examines the current state and the likely future of Python integration within the general cyber security and digital investigation field. In addition, we take a look at a Python script that extracts and carves data from the popular .MP3 file ID3 headers. The reader is then challenged to integrate this script with one or more leading forensics platforms discussed in this text or using other source.

I certainly hope you enjoyed this book, and it has inspired you to not only develop Python scripts but to also integrate those innovations into existing platforms and share them with your colleagues. I look forward to hearing from you.
Warmly, Chet Hosmer
e-mail: cdh@python-forensics.org
Twitter: @PythonForensics
Linkedin: https://www.linkedin.com/in/chethosmer

Additional Resources

[1] ID3 Tag Standard, http://id3.org.

Index

Note: Page numbers followed by *f* indicate figures and *t* indicate tables.

Printed in the United States
By Bookmasters